LIVING NAKED AND FRUGAL

A Handbook for Parsimonious Nudity

Paul Penhallow
with Marilyn Lovell

Loompanics Unlimited
Port Townsend, Washington

This book is sold for informational purposes only. Neither the author nor the publisher will be held accountable for the use or misuse of the information contained in this book.

Living Naked And Frugal
A Handbook For Parsimonious Nudity

Published by:
Loompanics Unlimited
PO Box 1197
Port Townsend, WA 98368
Loompanics Unlimited is a division of Loompanics Enterprises, Inc.
1-360-385-2230

Photographs by Marilyn Lovell, Nancy and Darrell Casey, Fred and Lana L. VanNest. Cover photo by Nancy and Darrell Casey.

ISBN 1-55950-165-0
Library of Congress Card Catalog 97-72031

Contents

Preface i

Foreword iii

Part I

Chapter One: The Basics 1
Yes, Dorothy, there are plenty of places to go naked, and most of them are not in Kansas

Part II: The Nuts and Bolts

Chapter Two: Accept Yourself 13
Why would you want to live naked?

Chapter Three: Respect Others 25
How do you live naked with others?

Chapter Four: Live Simply 37
How little can you spend on living naked?

Chapter Five: Relax Daily 59
How do you use your naked time?

Appendices

Appendix I : The Options...71
Directory of campgrounds, facilities, phone numbers

Appendix II : Bibliography...83
A *Barely* Sufficient Library

The Four Laws of Nudism:

Accept Yourself

Respect Others

Live Simply

Relax Daily

"What spirit is so empty and blind, that it cannot grasp the fact that a human foot is more noble than the shoe and human skin more beautiful that the garment with which it is clothed."

– Michelangelo

Dedication:

This book is dedicated to George and Mary Robinson, practical leaders of American Nudism, and is aimed at all those who want to march to the beat of a different drummer — without wearing a uniform!

PREFACE

Michael Hoy, President
Loompanics Unlimited
P O Box 1197
Port Townsend, WA 98368

Dear Michael Hoy,

In January, 1996, Dr. Robert A. Holm wrote to you concerning the development of his book, "*Living Naked.*" You responded, "Sounds good to us. Please send an outline and sample chapter!"

In February, Dr. Holm, AKA Paul Penhallow, went off to the Mid-Winter Naturist Gathering in Florida, came home with what seemed like a bad cold, ended up in the hospital where murmurs of "Leukemia" began. He immediately called for his laptop and began a concentrated effort to get "*Living Naked*" together.

Of course, he didn't plan to settle for "an outline and sample chapter." He wanted to send you the full manuscript, complete with graphics, tables and typesetting. He had developed, edited and published the *Syracuse Naturist Gazette*, and enjoyed both the writing and the preparation for printing.

By the end of April, the diagnosis was a definite "Acute Leukemia" with three to nine weeks to live. Talk about giving "deadline" a new meaning. (He could have chosen to die earlier and longer via chemotherapy, but we'll save that for my sequel, *"Dying Nude.")*

The book remained a major focus through those last weeks of his life; he died May 21, 1996. I was honored with the position of Crone to his dying, and he also charged me specifically with the job of cleaning up what he had written and getting it off to you, as ready as possible for publication.

I am so pleased to have worked with you to present this one of his last works.

SUNcerely,
Marilyn R. Lovell

Robert Holm, AKA Paul Penhallow, circa 1993.

Foreword

Naked

1: lacking covering: uncovered: as (a) not wearing, covered by, or protected with, clothing: nude (b) inadequately or partially clothed, esp. so as to be socially unacceptable.

4: devoid of concealment or disguise as (a) outspoken or straightforward: presented without reserve or embellishment (b) open to view : plainly manifest

Nude

1 (a) lacking some essential particular: being without consideration: naked, unsupported (b) Roman law : having no cause

2 devoid of some natural, conventional, or customary covering, furnishing, or adornment

3 (a) devoid of clothing: unclothed (b) undraped — used of an artistic representation of a human figure.[1]

I use the word "naked" in this book as expressing more exactly the forceful, intentional state of being without clothing, rather than the supposedly more politically correct but passive and neutral word "nude." As you can see from the Brittanica definitions, with

---

[1] *Encyclopedia Brittanica.* 1973.

their Victorian roots, both are assumed to be negative, pejorative states or conditions. We who live naked know better.

I use "naked" much for the same reasons of style and honest communication as when referring to my own body parts, I use the honest Anglo-Saxon word "cock" rather than "penis." In deference to the sensibilities of some, I avoid the use of "cunt" rather than "vulva" because of its historical pejorative use (and especially so when I am apt to get a swift punch from any of my liberated women friends who happen to be within reach at the time).

AMERICAN CIVIL LIBERTIES UNION OF FLORIDA POLICY

— Approved by the Board of Directors
October 16, 1993 — St. Petersburg, Florida

The Right to Dress

1. The ACLU contends that the Constitution protects the right to choose one's personal appearance. Government regulation of personal appearance is fundamentally inconsistent with the right of expression, personal and private autonomy protected by the Constitution.

This right of personal appearance necessarily includes the right to dress or undress. Accordingly, laws that prohibit mere nudity are incompatible with these rights.

2. The Florida ACLU rejects the view that government may prohibit conduct merely because such conduct is offensive to others. The government must demonstrate a legitimate and compelling interest in the regulation or prohibition. The fact that nudity or style of dress may cause offense to others is not a legitimate governmental interest for this purpose.

WANNA LIVE NAKED? DO IT, DAMMIT — you'll never experience the true limits of your freedom until you take action!

CAUTION: some of the observations in this book are based on single incidents or what's apparently reliable hearsay evidence. They are included so you don't wander off the rose garden path and get all bent out of shape if you find yourself in the ol' briar patch. For a true nudist, this can be a painful experience in more ways than one.

To any weekend nudists or resort owners who pick up this book and respond a little tenderly on some of its points, all I can say is: "If the foo shits, wear it."

Part I
Chapter One
The Basics

It's a bright, warm morning, and you wake to the sounds of birds and the burble of a brook in the valley. You get up naked, walk to the outdoor shower, feel the hot, refreshing spray and watch the morning mist rise off your body as you dry out in the warming rays of the rising sun, standing in your full, naked, personal glory. You may be the first person in camp to be awake on this new morning, and the only one to watch the gentle fog rise, and the dew on the clover sparkle. You have some sense of what it would be like to live naked and greet every morning with this same joy and freshness. You say, deep down inside yourself, "Yes! This is for me!"

There are many, many places where you can live naked. Not one of them is the same as any other; ownership, operations, attitudes, reputations all vary tremendously from one resort or club to another. The facilities range from rugged seasonal sites owned by "any old fart with forty acres" to luxury, full-service trailer parks and on up through the stratosphere to luxury condos or permanent conventional homesites in "clothing-optional" subdivisions and developments. At less expensive levels there are seasonal tent or travel-trailer sites, unpowered rustic tenting for pop-up trailer gypsies, and even pull-though sites for your $150,000 Pace Arrow land-going yacht. The unique feature of all of these options is that they are on resort or club properties where part of the deal is the freedom to go naked.

2

The clothing lock on our minds is so rigid that, except for skinny-dipping a few times when we were growing up, we have seldom if ever heard of, or considered the possibility of nude recreation, and one is surprised to learn of the extensive array of nude beaches and resorts which are in daily use serving thousands and thousands of American citizens every weekend. Many of the uninitiated would be astounded to learn that it is both legal and accepted to go naked in a social group at many beaches and resorts in the United States.

Although most citizens have a lack of specific knowledge about nude recreation and living opportunities, they are, in accord with the founding principles of this country, quite tolerant of others living naked. In fact, public surveys consistently show that over seventy percent (70%) of Americans are willing to let others go naked on beaches and in resorts as long as the areas are properly designated and managed so as not to interfere with the "sensibilities" of clothed citizens.

The honest advantages and pleasures of living naked are all so palpable, specific, real, practical, predictable, and positive. Why are all the supposed disadvantages so vague, counter-factual, or just plain false? Chalk it up to ignorance, prejudice, bias, social taboo and superstition.

The beauty of joining an established resort is that the owner has already, by and large, fought the battles with the local suck-o-crats and county Gestapo and established his right and license to protection and operation of a "naked zone" within his private club or resort property.

The common features of all these different opportunities for living naked are that they are nearly all cheap, peaceful, secure, and allow a remarkable degree of personal freedom and anonymity.

CHEAP — The clubhouse, swimming pool, hot tub, sauna, tennis courts, and hiking trails at many nudist resorts are often aimed at serving a large weekend clientele and are available to long-term residents at bargain rates. Of course, if you really want and can afford to pay top dollar at a nude social-entertainment-disco-fast-lane resort you can find those also. Even at that, where else can you enjoy your drinks and music in the buff, dance naked until the wee hours, and then hit the hot tub on the way from the dance to your own digs a short walk away?

PEACEFUL — Even for clubs with hundreds of permanent sites and thousands of members, most club members typically use their resort privileges from Friday evening to Sunday afternoon, and the rest of the time the "true nudies" have the place to themselves. Nearly all of these resorts are in remote locations on dead-end roads in prime outdoor and natural recreation environments. Many sites abound with birds and other wildlife, from rabbits and squirrels to deer or bear, and there's at least one resort I know of with fairly frequent moose sightings!

Being natural as a part of nature is truly awesome. Living and working in such an environment is a different world from trying to pack your freedom into tight, occasional weekend visits.

SECURE — Theft and pilferage are somehow just not compatible with living naked. Once inside the gate, locks are often forgotten as sort of "clothing for doors." A fair degree of caution with regard to valuables in your car in the public parking area on a busy transient weekend is probably just common sense, but in general you and your property are completely safe.

I live in a trailer with seven computers, two guitars, a fine art collection, a fair sound system and rather good classical CD collection, together with beaucoup other useful stuff, and I often leave the site for days or weeks without even bothering to lock the door. Try that in New York City — or even Des Moines! The major use of locks, or even ordinary door latches, around a nudist resort is to keep young kids or critters from wandering through your digs. I got a little careless one summer, and that fall found my boots, my couch, even the center of the toilet paper rolls, filled with acorns and shells from the local chipmunks!

A nudist resort is, also, a very small community. Club rules are direct and justice is swift so the possibility of losing all the unexcelled benefits of living "sky clad" is a great deterrent to anyone messing around with other folks' stuff. Nobody is going to make even minor transgressions of the law on the chance that they would come to the attention of the local gendarmes and blow their cover. "Undercover in a nudist resort," now THAT'S a concept to think about for a while.

ANONYMOUS — The one pervasive attitude giving most nudists a measure of anonymity with regard to other nudists is the current paranoid structure of nudism in the United States. Of course, you have to have positive identification for the owner of the resort, but the average person you meet at a resort still lives with clothing most of the time, and practically all of these will tell you they are absolutely convinced that they would lose their jobs and be tarred and feathered and run out of town if their bosses or families found out they were nudists. Now, since you, yourself, have already come out of the closet (and left your clothing behind), these problems won't bother you. This misinformed attitude of fear in others adds to the environment of privacy and anonymity within which you can relax, live and work.

You can, and will, naturally, develop warm friendships, share meals, chat poolside, have a few drinks or dance and hot-tub naked with folks, but it can be a long time or forever before you know the personal details about any of them, and if the occasional motor-mouth does want to dump their personal bag of shit on you, you can deal with it in your own way. If you respect other people's paranoia, they will respect yours.

Strangely enough, you can get naked and become invisible.

Look around the office or up and down the street and ask yourself, honestly now, how many of these folks would you recognize if they had no fancy dresses or sharp suits, makeup or toupees, and were laid out stark naked alongside a swimming pool with twenty or so other folks like a row of sea lions at La Jolla? Whom would you know? Damn few, betcha.

The same thing works to your advantage when you, too, get naked. You drive through the security gate at your local nudist resort with YOUR car, wearing YOUR clothes, and sign in with YOUR ID. Then you park YOUR car, toss YOUR clothes in the back seat, grab YOUR towel, take three steps from the car and *Voilà!* You are invisible. The instant you separate from all your tags and labels you become anonymous, just another plain face (or bare ass) in the crowd. You become so totally yourself that your "good buddies" who depend on shields, labels and uniforms (whether military or corporate) would do a classic Marx brothers triple-take and still have to ask if that human in the buff in front of them was really you. We are so conditioned to tags and labels that a real human, naked, totally unique, simply doesn't compute, so our brain switches off and we start with a complete blank page. It's like putting on a workman's beret in the streets of Paris and instantly becoming undifferentiable from the rest of humanity. Here you take off your pants or dress and immediately become part of the crowd.

Remember the old classic film, *The Invisible Man*, with Alex Niven? After his drinking the potion and becoming bodily invisible, we were treated to a titillating mental exercise of watching Alex undress "before our eyes" and carefully lay his clothing aside. Now, in your filmic imagination, you have a naked man moving about before you. But without his clothing, he can't be seen at all!

When I was having regular open house for the local nudists at my apartment in Syracuse, I got to know and visit comfortably with a roly-poly cherubic middle-aged gentleman who mixed well with everybody and in general shared with us all in just hanging out naked, sunbathing on the balcony, joining in our potluck nude dinners and even exchanging a few stress-relieving back rubs on our communal massage table. Then one day when I answered the door to let in a member, there was this totally ferocious looking dude in a dark blue suit with a distinct bulge under his left armpit and a much-better-than-average communications pack on his belt. He acted like I should know him, but it wasn't until he had laid the shoulder holster on the closet shelf and started to disrobe that it registered with me who this was. It was my roly-poly cherub friend in mufti!

"What the hell do you do for a living anyhow?," I asked.

"Oh, I'm a federal Marshall and specialize in transporting dangerous criminals cross-country," he nonchalantly replied.

Like wow! A naked fed bounty hunter. Let Ragnar Benson picture that!

The real point is that, naked and free, you can relax, let down the force shields and start to be, really be, yourself.

How many naked places are there? If you use the standard directory for nudist resorts, there are over two hundred nudist resorts in the United States which are attended by about 60,000 nude recreationists. This doesn't count the additional nude beaches and traditional skinny-dipping spots, and the many, many private nudist resorts and clubs which are not members of the national organization. My rough guess is that if you add the smaller, private nudist clubs and resort communities, you come up with around 2,500 sites, located in practically every state of the Union. For some of these locations and addresses for both individual resorts, and for The Naturist Society (TNS) and The American Association for Nude Recreation (AANR), see Appendix I.

Some of the commercial services and computer disks being sold which purport to give such directory information are known to be woefully out of date, so the membership organizations, such as AANR and TNS, and their publications, are the most dependable source of current information.

Now, within this broad set of choices scattered from Quebec to California, from Washington State to Florida, there has to be one or several convenient spots where you could slip in and retire or relocate cheaply and comfortably and you, yourself, live naked! Before we review the kinds of "you" that could find living naked a life of creative freedom in the later chapters of this guidebook, let's look at some general facts about living naked in the United States.

To be a full-time resident in a nudist resort you have to have, first of all, a full club membership. In addition to that, you will need to have the price of whatever shelter you purchase, whether a simple tent trailer or a condominium, and site lease costs. These leases can be short-term rentals, seasonal, or permanent. As in any full-time living situation you will have utilities such as gas, power, and telephone bills, and the other maintenance costs for your mobile home or whatever other sort of palatial chicken coop you've arranged for yourself. However, these costs can be startlingly moderate.

In Syracuse, New York, I had a two-room apartment in a downtown high-rise for which I paid $675 a month. My fees for a whole year at the resort where I now live are $1600. That is, I am living in a three-bedroom, two-bath trailer, and for a full year's access to all the facilities of a luxury resort I am paying less than three months' rent on my old one-bedroom apartment. And I'm living naked!

These are all generalities. It seems reasonable that somewhere in all these hundreds of clubs, resorts and thousands of mix-and-match living options there is one that could fit you like a silk kimono — but it might be well to take a brief pause and see how you, the unique one, relate to some practical parts of living naked.

Before starting the next section of this guidebook, fill out the following questionnaire for your own reflection and review.

How many hours a day are you nude?

Is your home or apartment a "clothing-free zone"?

Do you get naked as soon as you enter your home, or as soon as the garage door closes and you get out of your car?

Are you naked mostly alone or in a group of roommates, family or friends?

Do you work, write, read naked? (That you sleep "au natural" is a given.)

Do you drive naked? Under what conditions?

Are you self-employed, retired, or do you have a small income that could finance your new, naked, frugal life style?

Do you, or could you, work out of your home or telecommute, or arrange your schedule to make time away from home in the clothed world less and less?

Are you free to relocate? Are you married? With kids? If so, is your family really familiar with or willing to take the risk of living naked?

Are you independent by nature? Can you do without vigorous social interaction for days at a stretch? Do you (a) like to be around folks but not necessarily always, (b) like to be around others only when you want to share or have mutual needs but otherwise love working and being by yourself, or (c) are you an extreme hermit who doesn't care if you ever see another person in the whole world (at least until the wounds heal)?

Have you ever been to a nudist resort?

For more than three times in any year?

For a total weekend or week-long stay?

Do you do your own cooking and laundry?

Do you have general good health with no chronic medical conditions requiring frequent specialist or clinical visits?

Do you have any experience in the small repairs associated with maintaining a home, trailer, or boat?

Now, in light of your actual experience and the reflections that you have just listed, what are some of the most positive things you would like to get from living naked full time in a nudist resort?

With this general overview of the tantalizing possibilities that you, too, could be living and creatively functioning in a clothing-free, quiet, secure, creative and productive environment, let us look at a few practical nuts and bolts which you might find useful in putting together your dream.

These practical "how-to"s are arranged according to four general laws of nudism which damn near everybody I've talked to says are pretty universally acceptable as a sensible basis for living (and especially for living naked).

Those four laws are:

1. Accept Yourself;
2. Respect Others;
3. Live Simply;
4. Relax Daily.

What we want to do for ourselves now is to go over the same four laws and add the word "naked:"

1. Accept Yourself Naked;
2. Respect Others Naked;
3. Live Simply Naked;
4. Relax Daily Naked.

Makes a difference, doesn't it?

In getting around in naked society, you should be aware of some of the jargon related to the national nudist organizations, The Naturist Society (TNS) and the American Association for Nude Recreation (AANR), formerly the American Sunbathing Association (ASA). These organizations have been operating for over forty years and have about 100,000 members in the United States. TNS arose out of the "free beaches" movement in the '60s and is primarily concerned with public access to designated nude beaches. AANR is a network of entrepreneurs and owners concerned with private commercial nude or "clothing-optional" resorts.

There was probably a time when it would have been pretty fair to characterize TNS as the laid-back, nude-beach hippies and AANR as the Neanderthal fenced-in straights. Those extremes have somewhat mellowed, although the AANR clubs are still the self-advertised bastions of conservatism, at least publicly, and the TNS folks are much more pluralistic and tolerant in their view of Life, the Universe and Everything.

Since living naked in a nudist resort involves both your club membership and your site lease, one of your growth challenges (read that as pain in the ass) will be the long-term development of trust with a specific camp owner or club membership committee (more of that under "respect others" later).

Another general fact. If you are a single man and want a woman, you've got to bring your own. Women, especially single women, are rare at nudist resorts, and sometimes (horseshit — damn near always) couples talk mostly with couples and women are often treated like a male chauvinistic piece of property and guarded by their men with all the fervor of a banty rooster watching over his hens, even when both members of the couple are quite happy to be completely nude in a social setting. Those women who are independent enough to be at a nudist resort on their own are likely tired of the bar scene and the losers to be found there and want fervently to be left alone. If you try to push, you will likely precipitate a complaint to the boss and find yourself looking at the outside of the gate.

Couples, families or single women (with well-disciplined children especially) are like found gold to any resort owner and can expect a full red-carpet treatment, discounted rates and other preferential perks. Sorry, guys, that's life in the big bad world. No doubt there is a singles prejudice. However, if you are simply into getting naked and relaxing alone this shouldn't bother you. The background scenery of a couple dozen well-tanned, naked couples and women doesn't hurt the creative relaxation process a bit.

Tolerance for gays and gay couples also varies greatly from one resort to another, with, in general, the larger and more businesslike operations being much more tolerant in lifestyle areas. Currently active gay naturist groups include:

IMEN (International Men, Enjoying Naturism, Inc.) and GNI (Gay Naturists International), with more active local groups than you might expect to find (See Appendix I). I personally know of two fine clubs with permanent seasonal and transient sites in the Commonwealth of Pennsylvania that are specifically for gay men, and another that quite happily includes both lesbians and gays in their membership. If that's your bent, you actually may find acceptance in a gay club or resort an easier battle than that of a single straight male trying to get accepted at a so-called "family-oriented" resort. Although the permanent residence opportunities for the gay nudist may still be limited, gay clubs represent the fast-est-growing, most affluent segment of nudism in America today. There are ample opportunities for any individual lifestyle, from conventional to radical, to live naked.

Part II: The Nuts and Bolts

Chapter Two
Accept Yourself

The last time you were naked in a social group was... when? Quite likely it was when you ran out from under the table at momma's dinner party or trotted across the alley to inspect the neighbor's flower garden in your altogether and momma dutifully whopped your bare behind and threatened you with the end of the world if you were ever caught without clothing again.

What did this teach you about your body and yourself? Shame, loathing, dread, ignorance, secrecy? So there might be a bit of returning, and bit of relearning, and bit of restarting to do here for most of us to reclaim our own individualities and, along with that, our own natural bodies. In a very real sense it is regaining personal control over our own bodies and making our own choice as to whether we are forced to cover our bodies in the "rags of shame" or walk "sky-clad" and accept our bodies as good and beautiful; not perfect, beautiful.

That you are even considering living naked probably means you are a good way down the road to accepting yourself as you, and rejecting all the bags of false guilt and burdens of rejection this society heaps on us from the day of our birth. I won't belabor the point, but once you've been inoculated against media manipulation, the appeals to make you "smell BETTER, look YOUNGER, REMOVE this, or CHANGE this, or COVER UP something else" so you can become "good, popular, sexy, or socially accepted" all begin to appear to the new you as something between laughable and nauseating.

The nude life in brief(s).

Chances are by now you know pretty well how far you have gotten and how much further you are likely to get. Illusions are fading. *The Courage to Be*[1] has become to you a warm and glowing hope in an otherwise cold and crushing scene. Some of us have gone through all that and rediscovered the warmth of now, the peace of accepting, the reality of sense and pleasure and thankfulness for each small daily pleasure. You are you, you start where

---

1 *The Courage To Be,* Tillich, Paul. London, The Fortana Library, Sixth Printing, 1969.

you are. You have the desire to open new doors, let in the sunshine and fresh air, and walk once more upon the earth as a free person, LIVING NAKED!

In the questionnaire you answered earlier, you noted where you were with regard to already living naked. Becoming more comfortable with yourself and your body and being naked at home is a great step forward.

Do you want to know a great secret? The simplest, cheapest health aid, both physically and mentally, when living naked, is, believe it or not, MIRRORS. Huge, full length, wall-sized mirrors wherever! You see movement, you see yourself from all angles, you learn to accept, day by day the familiar image of the real you, and the mirrors become your friends rather than your critics.

You can buy light-weight mirrored Lexan (polycarbonate) sheets in 4 x 8 foot sheets at specialty plastic-supply houses for less than $100 a sheet and have the shop cut them to order or saw them yourself with a regular circular wood saw. The pieces bend around corners for handling and the safety of having plastic rather than glass, combined with their light weight, makes handling and mounting, using ordinary edge clips, a simple matter. If you decide to move them someplace else, it's no big job to do so. If you can't do that right away, pick up two or three 12″ x 48″ pre-framed mirrors from Wal-Mart. If you prop one of these mirrors vertically, with the bottom about eight inches from the wall, and step back five to ten feet, you can see ALL of yourself, from head to toe. Try them across the living room, at the end of the hall, wherever. Thus the mirrors become your friends, greeting you in the morning, reflecting the sun rays on your bare skin as you walk into the living room or back from the kitchen, showing you how to stand a little straighter, move a little smoother, almost automatically pulling in your gut or lifting your chin for your "audience" of one. I am convinced I lost part of a rather noticeable paunch, and straightened out a "scholar's slouch," not by beating on one small innocent part of my flesh, but by simply looking daily at my whole self and visualizing how and in what positive ways I wanted to change. Although by no means a member of the "youth cult," it is still an ego trip for me when, at over sixty, someone around the pool will mistake me for a person in their late forties or early fifties.

Note how the Puritans and Calvinists have given mirrors a bad name, and how the press has, sheep-like, followed the trend with cheap shots such as "the pervert arrested was found to have three copies of *Playboy* magazine and huge mirrors in his house." What these religiofanatics are fighting is not vanity, but the limitless power of self-knowledge. The fascist slave drivers realize that if they can keep us from ever really knowing who we are, then they can make us believe we are whatever they want us to be in order to feed their own lust for power. Just remember, as Lee Baxandall of The Naturist Society says, "Clothing makes the man — into a tool of the State."

If, after living naked around the house for a few weeks, you still feel a little trepidation about really accepting yourself, take a full length mirror and stand naked in front of it (with the lights on!). Now, is that person really you, or just somebody else's body with your head nailed on top? Can you honestly, deeply look at that whole, naked person, from all angles, and say, "Yes, that is me and I can hug my own body and accept this warm sack of skin with those arms and those legs and those bright eyes as my very own bag for now?"

As a real topper, if you have any doubts, jump up and down and laugh or dance naked in front of the mirror. Honest, nobody's looking, and besides a good part of living naked is being a bit more childlike and spontaneous. Dumb stuff, you might say, for grown, mature (so-called) adults? Kids love to do it. Try it yourself. You might be surprised at the results, and laugh a lot!

OK, OK, so you jumped the fence and went through your personal hoops and you are sure you are OK, even if the rest of the world is crap. What next?

The following chapters will give you some hints for surviving in the nude jungle. The examples are largely in temperate, but moderate, climates. Once you get located and the lifestyle is working for you, it is easier to move within the network, if that is what you want to do. California and Florida are special cases, and the "let's retire to Florida" gambit seems to me to be both risky and possibly a lot more expensive than you need to obtain most of the same benefits elsewhere.

First, however, let's take a slight side trip into another area of self-acceptance with a brief review of your personal talents and resources. The people I have in mind for this adventure are those independent creative people such as yourself who might, for example, consider a working retirement or mid-life relocation to someplace like Triangle Park, North Carolina, or a two-residence, summer-winter situation, rather than a full-time subtropical paradise. If you decide on the bipolar solution, I will leave the tax machinations of a second residence and all that to those who take masochistic glee in doing battle with the IRS, and will just stick to the other practical facts for now.

If you are like me, you have lived with feet of snow, ice and subzero cold for what seems like centuries, and paradise is any place where the accepted sign of community involvement is NOT a pair of snowshoes hanging in the garage.

Sensible "aboriginal savages" get along, by and large, on no more than 3 or 4 hours of work a day to supply all their bodily needs. Are they that much smarter than we? You artists, consultants, yuppies, dinks, retirees into home businesses or telecommuting: — remember you don't want to be RICH, you want to be FREE. As Ben Franklin said, "He who spends a penny less a day than he earns is happy; he who spends a penny more a day than he earns is in misery." Trading a clothed treadmill for a naked one doesn't make a lot of sense, although it cuts down on the cost of cloth.

Living naked is being totally yourself, and if you are not or cannot be yourself, then just get a cheap trailer in some dirty, noisy, 2x4 ticky-tacky clothed trailer camp with *"Arbeit Macht Frei"* posted over the gate and forget about living naked in a secure, free, creative clothes-free environment. For those who might not remember, *"Arbeit Macht Frei"* is German for "Work makes you free," and was inscribed over the gate to Buchenwald, the Nazi death camp.

Exercise for Accepting Yourself Naked

For basics: Get naked more around your home. If it is impractical, impossible, or just too damn cold to get naked, wear something non-conventional, such as a woolen poncho, just a sweatshirt, or a blanket with snaps to hold it in place. This looser cover-up lets the energy flow more freely under the cloth and provides a feeling of "naked beneath our clothing"[2] as a step toward truly living free of clothing. The purpose here is to break the thoughtless habits of conformity, examine your real needs, and find functionality. There is really no sense to the layer after layer of stitched and sewn, knitted, belted, buckled, strapped, zipped and hooked-up garments that we HABITUALLY wear.

Truth in Labeling: "Caution, the Surgeon General has found that this garment is one of a class of manufactured items which are known to be habit-forming and detrimental to your physical, psychological, and economic health."

Another thing you can do is expand your naked envelope. Search out the old local skinny-dipping holes where it is reasonably safe to strip down and sunbathe out of sight without getting hassled when-

---

[2] *Naked Beneath Our Clothing,* Veltheim, John. Union Hall, VA, PaRama, 1994, p13

ever a sunny day comes along. Bring up the topic of skinny-dipping in casual conversation. Folks are willing to discuss old skinny-dipping spots and their experiences and you might even be able to make contact with some equally skin-tolerant people that way. Check Baxandall's *World Guide to Nude Beaches and Recreation* for skinny-dipping spots. You'll be amazed what you will find within an afternoon's drive of almost anywhere. If there is a group of regulars at any of your local nude beaches and they have formed a group to protect and enhance that local beach, certainly support them. If you are at all into that sort of social action, get involved in their information and lobbying activities.

Drive naked in the country in the evening or even during sunny days when the difference between a guy without a shirt and a guy driving starkers is impossible to discern in a moving car. A woman wearing a long blouse or sweat shirt and nothing else is also unlikely to get hassled. However, you'd better plan your passing and contact with the 18-wheelers. They don't have those little windows in the passenger side door for any OSHA-regulated purpose; they give a passing truck driver a bee-line view of your crotch. Keep the CB cranked up when driving naked in trucker territory so you can keep track of the scuttlebutt.

Remember, the objective of nudity around home, sunbathing and skinny-dipping, and driving nude is to experience the personal freedom and wholeness of your body out in the sun and air and allow you to climb that psychological ridge and get over the pass to that new country where, contrary to our current conditioning, it feels ODD to wear clothes and NATURAL to be naked — then you will *really* be on your way!

You can get a bit too comfortable about it. One afternoon I was driving back naked from a favorite skinny-dipping spot at Chimney Bluffs on Lake Ontario, cruising along down the four-lane highway on a warm sunny late Sunday afternoon when my brain suddenly triggered to the fact that I had just gone under the last underpass between open country and serious downtown. Oh, shee-it! A quick stop at the side of the four-lane to slip on my britches and I proceeded on home. I wonder what would have happened if I'd got all the way to the parking lot, stepped out, and walked up to the security desk on the way to my apartment, all the while equally oblivious of my "natural" state?

"Now, you see, Judge, it was just forgetful and totally inadvertent..."

Pay your dues and become a member of The Naturist Society (TNS) and the American Association for Nude Recreation (AANR). For eventually living naked, these memberships are a start to contacting like-minded folks who might help you with information and leads. If it isn't practical for you to become a member of AANR through a local club, you can get (or as of this writing you could get) an unaffiliated membership by calling or writing directly to AANR.

Read the publications that come with these memberships, a fine four-color magazine called *Nude and Natural* for TNS and a formidable newspaper-format *Bulletin* from AANR. Lee Baxandall's *World Guide to Nude Beaches and Recreation* is a must for expanding your personal knowledge and developing local opportunities for personal relaxation.

The publications of TNS and AANR are excellent sources of news on resort developments around the country, and in the case of *Nude and Natural*, on the international scene also. For the stateside site seeker, the *Bulletin* can be helpful with its local and regional news and its want-ads and properties-available section. You'll find a lot of possibilities listed there, although it seems that more than half the ads are from one very upscale resort (Paradise Lakes) in Florida. I'm not sure whether that's owner or broker speculation, high turnover in a ritzy district, or just plain sales talk, but if it looks interesting to you, of course, check it out.

I would also strongly suggest purchasing AANR's *North American Guide to Nude Recreation* for a big book of mouth-watering photos of many of the best nudist resorts in the United States and a detailed listing of their facilities. Even with the sales bias of the AANR guide, it still gives a nice, varied view of what many clubs look like from a "home and gardens" viewpoint. The sun doesn't shine every place all the time, of course, but the basics don't change, and even on a cool, rainy day the huge stone fireplace in the dining room at Avalon can be a comforting and comfortable spot to spend an afternoon.

You can phone in your orders for any of these books, and while you are waiting day by day for your first stuff to arrive, you might do some prospecting for the Naturist Society's *Nude and Natural* magazine, which is carried in the travel and recreation section of many Barnes and Nobles bookstores.

Don't scrimp on these up-front costs. Remember, you are looking to make a shift that will, in addition to saving you thousands of dollars a year, allow you to relax and live naked!

As you DO these things, the personal experiences and interesting reading will enhance your ability to ACCEPT YOURSELF and draw you further along the path toward living naked.

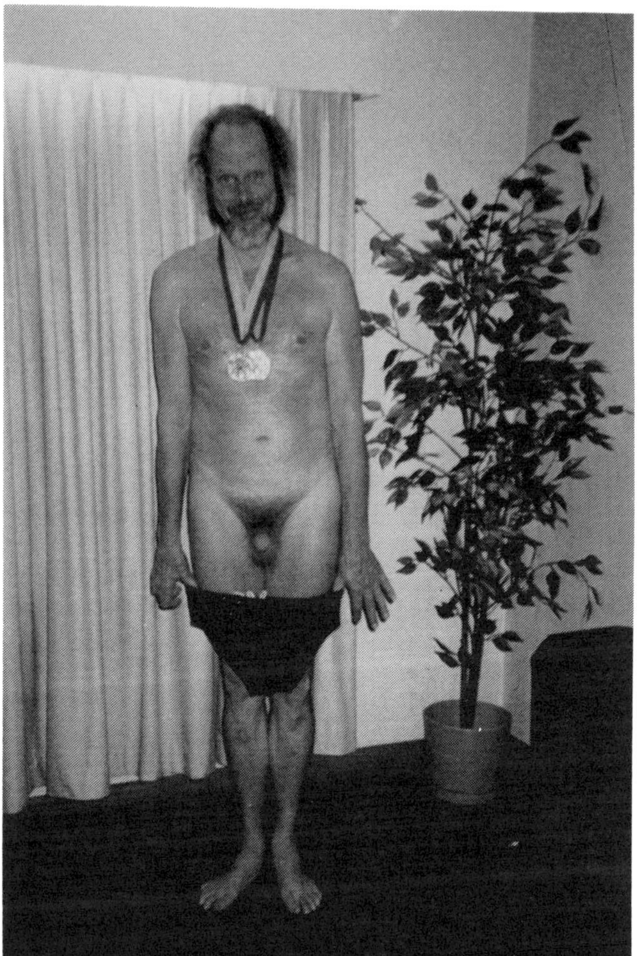

Take it off!

Take it all *off!*
(The gold medals were won in two diving categories at the Empire State Games.)

Chapter Three
Respect Others

You want to live naked, to be free, to create, or work, or just be, truly, yourself. To avoid the hassles of homesteading your own private nude area from scratch and allow yourself to take advantage of the established infrastructure and economies of living in an established resort, you have to consider your connections to other people.

It is at this point that you can begin to extend your individual self-acceptance and start to experience social nudism. Your reading and previous recreational nudist visits are part of your experience, but now you are shifting your focus from a relaxing day or two in the sun toward actually enjoying the freedom and benefits of full-time living naked.

By this time you are well on the way to living naturally and have a whole list of possible spots to visit and check out, and a current membership card in some national nudist organization such as TNS or AANR. The "things-to-do" section at the end of this chapter will give you some direct guidance as to locating and visiting nudist resorts as you look for a spot that suits (damn textile pervasiveness) you. A few hints, however, might be in order if you have never stripped buck nekkid and strolled nonchalantly into a swimming-pool area where there are a couple of dozen equally clothes-free people swimming and sunning themselves.

As a first-time visitor, you likely will move alongside the group lying out alongside the pool, establish cordial eye contact, and just hang on the edge of the group and settle down with a good book and a brew. See what others do.

You might have already had Social Skills 101, but if you've been chained to a workaholic treadmill for the past twenty years while the wife raised the kids, spent the money, and then grabbed everything and split, your recollections of exercising the social graces might be a bit faded and need to be slowly and carefully nurtured back to life. Wait to be included. There is a fair chance this might not happen on the first, or even the third, visit but waiting to be invited is a lot less risky than bulling in where you are not welcome and where your lack of social grace will be a long-standing mark against you.

If, contrariwise, you are into hermitsville like I am most of the time, the separateness is a boon, and sitting by the pool, using the outdoor shower, and reading in the sun, with a couple of dozen naked people swimming, sunning, and chatting in the background is a bonus. Don't take it too hard, but the vast majority of single men I have met on their first visit to a nudist resort are at absolute ground zero when it comes to social skills and interpersonal communication. You may be the exception, but then again you may not.

Oh, yes, the towel. Even as a nudist, you need one essential piece of cloth, a towel. Not just for drying off after shower or pool, but also for sitting on whenever and wherever you decide to park your bare butt. You don't want to see or squat on somebody else's skid marks, and nobody wants to wipe up your shit either, so you bring your towel with you wherever you go and always sit on the towel rather than the chair or lounge surface. Now there's a really practical application of the "golden" rule.

Sometime during the afternoon, as you are dozing off in the shade, someone will clang a bell or shout over the intercom the nudist's universal clarion call to battle, "VOLLEYBALL TIME!" Never played? Two left feet? Olympic gold medalist? Makes no difference. Do it for two very good reasons.

First, this physically active, traditional nudist-resort game makes you forget yourself and that you are naked (without removing the admiration you might feel for the lovely bodies playing in the game around you) and you begin to revel in just BEING. You are transformed into a leaping, yelling, laughing, healthy and happy person under the sun and sky, open to the breeze on your skin, and the feel of sweat on your back and sand under your feet (or, if you trip as often as I do, other parts of your anatomy as well!).

Second, in playing volleyball naked, you become a part, by action and osmosis, of the community of naked people, and after a couple of wild volleyball games and a hot shower, when you settle back on the sun deck it's more than likely that you will no longer be alone, but will be sharing your conversation and your brew with a small group of new-found naked friends. Go for it!

At this point, I offer my apologies to my women readers for a male-oriented diversionary section. What is the one objection raised by every non-nudist man when you mention casual social nudity in a group of men and women? You guessed it. "How's your woodie?" While the question about involuntary erections always comes up, the erections themselves hardly ever do. If we haven't been there, we often can't tolerate any ambiguity, so we fantasize on the basis of total ignorance.

I will give you my brief (without briefs) analysis of what happens to physical sexual responses in a nude social setting; nothing. You may not believe it, but it's true. I see more naked people in a week than most people see in a lifetime, and I have seen, over the past ten years or so, only one or two truly INVOLUNTARY erections, and those subsided within about ten minutes.

The analysis involves a combination of how many people are present, and whether nudity in that situation is relaxing or sexually stimulating. If there are only two people present, the focus of attention is on each other, and the chances are very high that stimulation will result, thank goodness! If you are in a larger social group of people that is occupied with ordinary things such as reading, eating, chatting, swimming, or simply lying out in the sun, the tension which might result from all of you being naked is spread out over the larger group, and a general feeling of heightened pleasure results which is much closer to relaxation than to stimulation.

By the way, if you really can keep it up for more than 15 minutes without physical diddling or a super mind-trip, then I know a woman or two who might want to get to know you better.

Now my observations on involuntary erections don't, of course, include the dozen or so manual or mental masturbators I have seen at nude conferences and resorts at the rate of maybe one or two a year. A few times I have observed masturbationists hanging around on the fringes of a social nude gathering in a resort and who, it was evident, were getting their rocks off with either their fingers or their fantasies. In each of these cases, the men tried to be secretive or surreptitious, did not disturb the general group, and were just ignored until they either wised up and found they didn't fit in and left, or they got over it and joined the group.

If you try any direct sexual display or solicitation inside a resort, or if you don't let your cock naturally relax, someone is apt to complain and you will be given the bum's rush in no uncertain terms and asked not to return. There is a quite efficient self-protecting blacklist at work among resort owners, so if you intentionally screw up at one location, chances are you will find the gate closed elsewhere also.

Sometimes when you are naked in a social group for the first time you may tend to retrogress toward the LAST time you were naked, and your thoughts and personality, even for a grown person, can get slightly tense and childlike.

Worry not. For every one I've encountered who is new to the scene, this phase passed quickly, usually evaporating in somewhere between ten seconds (Holy Toledo! It's great to be naked!) to a half hour or so ("Y'know, suddenly I realized I had forgotten I was in a group of naked folks, and it felt great just to be me.").

All of these great experiences are the same for weekend recreational nudists. What's different about you? You are a nude guerrilla prospecting for a place to live naked, so you have to stay more alert and be a bit more aware of the nuts and bolts of living full time in a nude community.

A few comments on dead ends. Sex and swinger's clubs, which abound, are unlikely to be good candidates for living naked. The temporary nature of their contacts, the part-time character of their lifestyle and the development of sex as a competitive sport do not allow for rational full-time living opportunities. I'm not knocking sex or swingers or their pleasures, I'm just pointing out sex is only a part (a very important part, of course) of a full life, and living naked is living WHOLE. There are a few nudist resorts with a distinct "party" atmosphere, but the ones most dedicated to hedonistic revels are, by and large, not good candidates for cheap, quiet, long-term residency. Great places to visit, but you probably wouldn't want to live there.

A nude community has many of the aggravations common to any small group, as well as a few redeeming virtues that can make the "small-town" horseshit more bearable. You may be disappointed to learn that most nudists, even those living as full-time nudist resort residents, don't live naked. Most, in fact, lead a sort of relaxed laissez-faire existence better described as "clothing optional." This is one case where the several pages of finely printed club rules are more honored in the breach than the observance thereof. The rules, if they exist, usually state that nudity is the preferred mode, weather permitting, but I see folks with street clothes on bopping around when I am personally quite comfortable naked. The nudity rule is, however, strictly enforced around the pool areas, hot tub, and the public recreation areas, like the clubhouse, at most resorts, so at least those areas are purely "nudist." The opposite extreme of enforcing goosebumps on all members by naked Gestapo agents is certainly worse than letting folks cover up when they feel like it.

If live and let live is your motto, some of the social factors can be less of a hassle. Be civil with all, but above all be yourself. You can be, if you wish, a functional hermit with only a courteous nod or "howdy" to those you meet on your walks along the trails or from the pool to the clubhouse. The pressure to "socialize" can vary widely from one extreme to the other. In one club I know, if you don't drink and party with the boys and their broads late into Saturday night you are really considered out of it. In another camp, some folks who live there are hardly ever seen, with no apparent backbiting about it, and in yet another club the attitude is open and receptive to both couples and singles to join in on whatever conversation happens to be in progress. So every resort has its own individual character and attitude. This sense of attitudes will be another result of your prospecting visits and travels, and will be invaluable as you start to shape your own future.

Many of us either grew up in the big city, or it has been so long since we've had to deal with this "small town," "high school" sort of situation, that it is long forgotten. In any nudist community there will be the cliques and claques, the gossips and needle-nosers, but if you are living naked, you can learn to live with, ignore, or even get involved with and enjoy this sort of social small stuff as you choose.

Beyond hermitsville, as you start to relax and reach out a bit on your weekends or longer visits, you will find that the following common courtesies apply naturally in a nude community: Don't schmooze around other people's trailers or campsites unless invited. The clubhouse, swimming pool, hot tub, and tennis courts are all fine public places to open up your shell a bit and develop contacts as you will, but many members are as interested in peace and quiet as you are, and their campsite, trailer, or cabin-condo is their private, personal Shangri-La. Besides, it's only common sense that if you see that trailer rockin', you damn sure don't want to go a-knockin'.

We all read suggestions like this and say, "Sure, fine, that's obvious." Good. Or we respond, "Everybody knows that." Or, "Of course, I always do it that way." Horseshit (for both me and for you). So read them over again. It's good to be reminded.

Getting along within the nudist community at any resort is important, but getting along with the owner is critical. You will be living naked in a very real sense. If your relations with the owner never develop, or turn sour, he or she can make your existence, even in the midst of paradise, a living hell. He can, without seeming provocation or recourse, cancel your membership in the club, thus shutting you off from your property or forcing you to hit the bricks on very short notice. Make sure you know and he knows continually that you respect his burdens and problems, adhere to all the rules, even if some of the little ones are pretty asinine, and pay every bill the same day it is given to you. No matter what else the big dude might be, he is in business for the money and he ain't stupid or he wouldn't own his own operation (well... every rule has its exceptions).

No matter what, however, the owner (or they if it's a couple, or if it's a nepotistic Byzantine fiefdom) is the one you GOTTA deal with, and if you can't get a mutual respect or working Mexican standoff at the very least, then you are the one who'll move. He owns the house, so don't even try to deal from the bottom of the deck; in many local areas, his is the only game in town.

We all resist change, and for many, many nudist club owners and especially for the "old-boy" cooperatives and committee-run establishments, it is an exceptionally novel and somewhat perverse concept that anyone would really want to live naked, full time, in, of all places, a NUDIST camp. Many of these folks relax and fully enjoy nude recreation on the weekends, for example, but never, ever go nude in their own homes. The old boys (many of whom are not male) are seriously dedicated to keeping their wagons circled and indulging in the typical closed-group gossip and petty politics in order to maintain the pristine nature of their weekend yuppie country club and mutual admiration society. If, in contrast to my own social limitations, you are a former sales VP and know how to deal with that sort of small-group political scene, bon appetít!

Don't get discouraged in your campaign to find your own personal Shangri-La or Xanadu. It IS out there, maybe just around the corner. However, there will be disappointments, mostly from where you expect them least: so-called nudists themselves.

Not that every (or most) resort owners are Simon Legree clones. One positive example I know of is George Robinson of Empire Haven Resort near Moravia, New York. This resort has a real gem of spirit that can make up for a lot of glitz and its rather cold winters. The philosophy of the owner-operator is key. This absolutely solid camp was founded forty years ago in virgin, potentially hostile territory by folks who really believed in and fought for nudism as a lifestyle. Their fight included a face-off with a hostile State Attorney General and an ancient, unenforced law against nudity, even on private property. This treasured attitude has been passed on to a second generation of owners. In addition to the proper philosophy, continuing good management has developed a first-class resort with large ceramic in-ground pool and sun deck, Finnish sauna, glassed-in large Jacuzzi, fine indoor clubhouse with library and snackbar, tennis courts, pétanque court, kids' playground, shuffleboard and tetherball for the youngsters, the ubiquitous sand volleyball court, and acres of forested trails for walking and meditation — and all naked country!

To develop your respect for others and reach out into the naked world, you can work on some of the ACTION SUGGESTIONS that follow.

Review your copies of Lee Baxandall's guide and the AANR directory for TWO types of locations: one group that is simply educational and aimed at expanding your perspective, and another group that includes real possible candidates, location, climate, and budget-wise, for your own version of living naked. If you write each of these resorts, mentioning your AANR or TNS membership, suggesting that you may be traveling that way in the near future, most will respond with a brochure and, if you ask for it, a price sheet which shows not only day fees, but costs for full membership and seasonal or permanent lease sites.

The initial list of AANR resorts in Appendix I, or your more detailed AANR Directory or Baxandall's *Guide* can be used to plan a longer loop trip with phone-ahead reservations to scope out a few prospective resorts, or simply to broaden your learning curve about the different personalities of the clubs, their owners, and some of their members. Some folks have tried to make one two-week blitz of a lot of resorts and clubs and then make a snap decision which they then have to live with for a long time. Not too bright. "Bet Not Thy Whole Wad."

Note that the directories often give phone numbers, not addresses or detailed travel directions. Expect a fairly extensive cross-examination before you get further travel directions or an OK to visit. If you just drive up to the gate you may or may not get in and undergo the once-over at the desk and a brief tour, but if your goal is a long-term relationship, calling ahead will grease the skids for a future courteous and respectful relationship. Your membership in a national nudist organization is a definite plus, and is normally considered a dividing line between gawkers and serious nudists. The Naturist Society (TNS) does not run any resorts, but a TNS card is accepted for both identification and some discount of fees at many resorts.

Your own naked comfort level will expand after a few club visits, so schmoozing your way in a more courteous and self-assured way through the gate will get easier and easier. Some clubs simply won't admit single men, some have a daily quota system, and others depend on the attitude of both the owner and yourself. If you are courteous and ask for advice, you can often get a trial waiver of the rules. Remember, you are dealing with a small shopkeeper who is conservative and defensive to a fault. These days there are more young entrepreneurs with forward-looking views, but more often than not, the owners are closer to what Ilsley Boone, a former Baptist minister who was an active organizer and promoter of early nudism in the United States, characterized as "any old fart with forty acres."

After a bit of prospecting, you will get "tuned in" to what you are looking for and what you want to avoid, so one weekend visit or even a day at a new resort can be enough to tell you if a spot is worth any further effort.

If you are not an experienced outdoors type or tent camper, you have a couple of options for these prospecting trips. Many resorts have rooms, cabins, or trailers to rent as a sheltered spot for sleeping, and this can give you one less thing to worry about during your visit. You can risk getting really close to nature and combine the challenges of nude recreation with trying to decipher the Japanese-English directions of how, in three hours or less, to set up a "one-minute pop-up tent." Our preference is to rent a room, ratty or luxurious, but waking up naked in your own sleeping bag and making your own morning coffee over an open fire is a totally unique way to experience nature.

At this phase in your campaign of nude discovery, contact local groups which may not own property, but still have leads on options in your area. You might even find a group of like-minded friends and start your own nudist cooperative, private lodge, or resort space. As I mentioned earlier, however, this can be a hard, slow way to go compared with the advantages of joining an established resort.

You want to live naked and relax and not have to take on all the headaches of pool and hot-tub maintenance, property ownership, zoning, and taxes. Respecting others in all those situations can cut into your time for living simply and relaxing daily!

The author relaxing daily.

Chapter Four
Live Simply

That's the real glory of it. If you can live cheaply and feed yourself, you become free, in whatever measure, from the daily time clock and treadmill. There is no "natural" schedule except the nights and days, the new to full moon, the solar equinox to solstice, or the annual cycle of sprouting and harvest. If you are living naked and wake up at 3 a.m. feeling alert and wanting to read, type, or work on some project or other, you can do it for as long as you want, and then, perhaps, roll back satisfied into bed around 7 a.m. and sleep until noon. Even then, if you feel the urge to experiment with different rhythms, you are completely free to start living those 25-hour days, getting out of bed an hour later every day and simply going to bed when you get tired. A Chinese proverb says that true wisdom consists of only two things: Eat when you are hungry, sleep when you are tired.

Wouldn't you like to sleep just a little longer every morning? Now will be your chance to do it.

So let's outline the practical aspects of setting up housekeeping as a full-time nudist, including shelter, food, washing, laundry, and furniture. Lots of these hints don't, of course, have to wait until you are living naked on site, but can be helpful for the newly independent person right where you are as you grow toward naked independence.

Most of my readers will be former suburbanite home owners who due to job change, divorce, or other reasons have been living for a time in an urban apartment with more or less dependence on the apartment and the city for services and infrastructure. The transitions to living naked can be simple, fun, and a source of a great feeling of individual independence and freedom, but in some cases need a considerable amount of thought and practice. Read that as, "it ain't always easy." "Life is so daily," Satchel Paige once commented.

Other options for the travel-minded are a decent pickup and a nice-sized fifth-wheel camper, or even a $200,000 land-going Taj-Mahal-on-wheels such as a "Sunseeker" or "Winnebago" or any one of many on the road. Fuel, parking, maintenance, and other expenses make me remember Mr. Morgan's comment about owning a yacht: "If you have to ask how much it costs, you can't afford one." The choice basically depends on whether your own style of living naked is going to be like mine, which is the "cheap-settled-productive" mode, or something more toward the "expensive-travel-tourist" end of the spectrum.

That brings us to the other option, gypsying or snowbirding. With your independent, retired, or self-employed telecom status it makes no difference whether you are in Hoboken, New Jersey, or West Palm Beach, Florida, so gear up your cabin tent or small travel-trailer (or prospect around for an affordable second trailer on a site further south) and check into your southern base on a long-term lease or rental spot until spring. Get naked, set up your laptop under the nearest palmetto bush, and find a friendly neighbor who'll trade you some land-line phone-connection time for whatever. If you get settled into more substantial winter quarters, of course, you can have an inexpensive seasonal phone line and all the amenities.

It is possible to scrimp even more by trucking your major kitchen stuff, such as the microwave, from one place to another, but I've found it more convenient to have roughly equivalent kitchen appliances in each place so that I can move back and forth more easily or just drop in and have everything I need right at hand. He who dies with the most microwave ovens wins. Right now I have a microwave oven in each of my two trailers, one in the old five-ton Mac tool truck I use for a wandering office and mobile nudist camp, and a smaller version I can dump in the car for short trips. As you can see, I am into the independence and food flexibility that a microwave oven offers, and it would be tough for me to get along without one. If you're into eating at the MacKingburger conveyor belt when on the road, then this will be one less complication you'll have to deal with.

Of course, if you are just popping south to avoid the cold until you can get back to your main base, your winter gypsy outfit can be fairly Spartan. In my case, however, I get antsy for my library and a substantial part of my computer gear, so "traveling light" doesn't come easily to me, and this eventually led to the use of the five-ton truck! Whatever the route, at each stop you can find a resort where you can relax among other nudists and get on with your other creative and relaxing activities while still living naked.

Shelter is as varied as your pocketbook. It is vital, not necessarily to get exactly what you want, but to get established inside an existing resort. The advantages of using the established structure of a resort and leaving all the multitudinous management headaches to the owner were mentioned briefly in the previous section on "BASICS," and now as you approach this decision for yourself, you may be able to see more clearly the advantages of letting someone else handle the hassles, especially when you consider what the owners of most resorts have already done to get licenses, zoning, add facilities, and provide a protected, enjoyable environment for nude recreation and naked living.

If you have pretty well decided on the resort, and you already have a full membership, and your visits and developing relationship with the owner seem to show you can growl respectfully at each other over the long haul, how do you make the move?

You might think I am emphasizing the negatives of owners, but believe me they are in positions of arbitrary authority and deserve the same respect (and contempt) as any other tax thug, cop, or Gestapo agent. Nevertheless, his position gives the boss access to information. Let's assume the boss knows a trailer or prime site is going to become available, and he's seen what an intelligent, upscale, fun person you are. I promise I won't tell him any different. Abe Lincoln's rule was to speak evil of no man and all the good he knew. That makes for a very short chat for some folks we know, but that's the way it is.

To return to your search for a trailer and/or site. Most of all, the boss needs to know that you are in a reasonable measure financially dependable. Remember, the amount of cash we are talking about here is really small for a person with the right priorities, and if you can't come up with that minimum on a dependable basis, you probably aren't going to make it in the "live-and-let-die" freedom of a nudist resort. You certainly don't have to be a Daddy Warbucks, and a lot of people I have met living in nudist resorts are in minimum-wage or less situations. If the boss thinks you would be a positive addition to his view of his resort, he will be happy to connect you with special opportunities. The alternative for him is eventually a vacant trailer full of chipmunks, looking progressively rattier and not contributing a dollar to his cash flow. There is a large turnover of trailers in most resorts due to people upgrading trailers or moving on and those who no longer feel that full site fees are justified for their weekend use of the club — whatever. Their change is your opportunity, and remember, by and large they are trying to get rid of what is an economic burden to them, and the bidding competition may not be very ferocious. It's nearly always a buyer's market, especially over a full season and in the winter or late fall when the rent comes due. Remember the old Dale Carnegie skit, "Who will pay the rent? I, Dudley Do-good will pay the rent!" (but take the trailer for my own).

My own preference is for a mobile home or trailer, both for convenience and relative stability, but if a trailer doesn't suit you, you can go either up- or down-scale (in terms of cash) from there. Some resorts have double-wide palaces nestled among the palm and orange trees, or luxury condos and self-built conventional homes at $100,000 and up. In the other direction there are many, many smaller trailers or even camper trailers or pop-ups on permanent or seasonal sites. These can range in cost from $5,000 for a fairly good-condition travel trailer to one fix-it tent-trailer I saw for sale for $300.

As in any purchase, you pay for what you get, but often there are problems and things to deal with regarding any particular trailer. Another option for summer sojourning is to set up an ample cabin-sized tent on a seasonal site, although if you need a dependable, dry, warm working environment for your craft or art work, or your computer, you need to think this one through. A yurt, anyone?[1]

Sometimes a so-called "seasonal" site can be made livable all year round, as long as you enjoy roughing it part of the year, don't mind hauling water from the main well, have an understanding owner, and the zoning rules allow for it. There are several year-round residents in a New York resort who get along fine this way, and I know of one couple who live year-round on a campsite in a small travel-trailer with electricity, but with water only part of the year. This is no big deal for them, since the clubhouse, common bathrooms, showers, and Jacuzzi are only a three-minute walk away. I imagine it can be a cold three-minute walk on a winter's morning, but they are living naked and to all appearances liking it just fine.

On some resorts, a permanent lease allows you to keep your trailer in place during the winter, but may not allow continuous oc-

---

[1] You can find out more than you want to know about Yurts by contacting: Pacific Yurts Inc., 77456 HWY. 99 S., Cottage Grove, OR 97424 (541)942-9435 FAX (541)942-0508 Internet http://www.yurts.com

cupancy due to local code restrictions. If you have a spare crying towel to lend, just ask any owner about his battles with the zoning board on "campgrounds" vs. "mobile home parks," vs. whatever other bureaucratic and inspection nightmares the local dumbocrats have aimed at him over the years.

Purchase situations can be quirky, however. The owner of one particular camp has his nose currently out of joint about one argumentative, messy old curmudgeon and another guy who's into a long-term gay partnership. Both of these members are reasonably tolerated by most of the other members, and have been members and leased their sites since long before the current owner took over. Since neither of these folks fit in with his current "image" for the camp, he has arbitrarily said he will no longer approve permanent site ownership by single men. Now, this is fiat veto control by a third party over a sale between separate private parties. It ain't fair and can severely jolt the salability and value of your own trailer, and unless you want to make a federal case out of it there's not a goddamn thing you can do about it. All owners have you by the short hairs, and the majority of them tend to look at you and the rest of their members as some sort of indentured personal property. The owner's flock is looked over with the same possessive, pseudo-protective paternalism that characterizes many a small independent Baptist church and its so-called pastor.

Some individual owners are well-known for their seeming arbitrariness. I know of one couple, athletic, strikingly handsome and articulate, college-educated and all, who had been going to a particular resort in the summers for several years. Eventually their views became too liberal for that owner and, in his typical European reticence and authoritarian modus, he gave no warning whatever until he tripped the guillotine and informed these folks they were no longer welcome at HIS campground. Out, no reason, no recourse. These resorts are often the only game in town for as much as four hours around, and folks willingly drive half a day just to spend a few hours out in the sun. The owner holds the key to the gate. Now, on the other hand, if you can get along with the owner, you can live there full-time and not have to drive at all!

My first trailer I bought foolishly, fully furnished in absolutely nauseating New Jersey rococo style and stuffed to the point where you could hardly breathe in the place, much less turn around or get any work done. I paid full asking price without bargaining, because I wanted to be in THAT resort at THAT time, was still working with a fair cash flow, and had the money in the bank and could afford it. The resort was only three hours from my current working location, and a very, very attractive friend lived full time at the same resort.

Damn straight that right now I wouldn't be able or willing to spot down $8,500 cash and not think twice about it. But even at that, what I got for the money was a fully equipped and installed two-bedroom, full-bath, kitchen and living-room trailer in the oak woods with an 18 x 24-foot redwood deck and a grassed lot, in a nudist environment with two 24-hour hot tubs (one indoor, one in an outdoor gazebo), an indoor heated pool, a sauna, an exercise room, two tennis courts and a long and lovely nature trail through the woods, all within a five-minute naked stroll from my door!

When you think about it, even though I paid roughly double the fair market value in that resort for an equal-sized trailer, I got, in larger terms, comparing options outside the resort, one hell of a bargain!

By the way, I tried selling off the furniture to my nudist neighbors. Bad move and waste of time! Since their ticky-tacky boxes were already full to the sills with the same trash, all I got was pooh-pooh and sales resistance. Most of the residents, with a few redeeming exceptions, were transplanted New Jersey suburbanites who had simply uprooted their corner of Hoboken and planted it down unceremoniously in the Poconos of Pennsylvania. Anyhow, I eventually made a few phone calls and donated the entire contents of blocky end tables and false leather swivel chairs and stuffed ottomans and large veneer bedroom sets et cetera ad nauseum to a local juvenile delinquents' social center. You should have seen the guys from the JD center as their truck chugged up the hill past a lovely nude couple just "layin' out" for the afternoon near their camper trailer having a couple of drinks and reading their books in the sunshine. The young "Christian evangelist" supervisor heading the work crew looked like he was going to have a chicken. Ah, yes, chalk up one more victory to real PUBLIC education.

The bulletin board at this camp usually has one or two trailers for sale at any time, which represent about one in twenty trailers openly advertised. We all know, of course, that almost anything is available if the price is right, but we are doing a little bottom fishing here, and special opportunities and fixup situations abound. Oh, by the way, the roof on the first place I bought leaked seriously and, in spite of a two coats of super-quality roof latex, continued to give me problems. Be warned.

The second trailer was a different story altogether. I was prospecting further south from my base in Pennsylvania, and looped down to the South Carolina border (a clean, nice resort there, but run by a rather straight-laced born-again couple and their thought police as a miniature version of John Calvin's Geneva. If you ain't sure what that means, see the *Encyclopedia Brittanica* under "Calvinism" or "Puritans"). In any event, the Myrtle Beach golf-plantation area was too rich for my blood. What is this obsession with whacking a defenseless little white ball around for most of the rest of your life as somebody's made-up version of heaven? Well, in a pluralistic democracy I can let them do their thing. After all, not everybody has to have three humming keyboards in front of his face to be happy either. One really unique feature about this resort in North Carolina was the small public subdivision outside the camp property that was, believe it or not, ZONED nudist, with several buildable lots available. But, like I said, this was not the time of life for me personally to put big bucks into a hole in the ground.

So I tooled back northward and stayed overnight at White Tail Park in the tidewater area of Virginia (for you Navy guys, about sixty miles west of Shit City). The boss and crew at White Tail (neat name for a nudist camp, don't you think — new untanned visitors are sometimes tagged as "bunny-tails" but as much in joke as seriousness) seemed friendly and tolerant and we'd had two or three previous contacts, one of which was while I was traveling with a woman who was well known and respected by the owner and his assistant, which certainly didn't hurt my reputation. Anyhow, we got to talking trailers at their morning staff meeting, and the owner said a former maintenance man had a trailer that was now vacant (this was in January) and he might be willing to part with it for around $3,000. This resort at this time was in a growth mode, adding sites to the mobile home side of the park, and it was evident the boss would welcome another full-time resident around the property. Always call him the boss. Nice guy or asshole, he is the boss, you're living on his turf, and it helps to always keep that in mind, although if you manage it right it need not crimp your style.

So, hey, let's take a look at this trailer under the helpful guidance of a retired marine scientist from Wood's Hole Oceanographic Labs. After looking over this extra-wide trailer with three bedrooms, kitchen, full bath and a half, paneled and mirrored living room with sliding glass patio doors on a full southern exposure, raised dining area with chandelier and kitchen, carpeted, tiled, fully skirted beneath with a good-sized outside work shed, and not a sign of roof leakage on a perfectly clean and level lot ... well, as you can imagine, I tried to keep the damned bullfrogs from leaping up and down in my gut as I calmly, ever so calmly, strolled back to the office. As off-handedly as I could, I opined that yes, it was a right nice trailer and I'd be most pleased to buy it. Right there, before witnesses, we restated the price and shook on the deal, and I sent the owner a check in full payment as soon as I got back north.

I now had two lovely trailers in prime vacation and recreation areas where I could live naked to my heart's content and had cut my rent costs by about half! Taking either trailer alone, you can see that the complete ANNUAL costs of living naked came to about

THREE MONTHS of living in a concrete coop where I had to cover up every time I set my foot out the door.

If you can live this cheaply, and live naked besides, does it really make sense to continue to work your ass off in a textile prison?

Now, back to reality: Whatever choice you finally make, you now find you have a roof over your head inside some corner of the clothes-free world. Congratulations!

Furniture

This business of furnishing a space to suit YOURSELF can be a big adjustment and a really freedom-expanding experience for a long-term marriage refugee who has been dominated by her spouse for decades, or some brow-beaten "good provider" who hasn't been allowed to move an end table in twenty years without a crisis-consensus-negotiation scene. Whatever YOU want, now is your chance to go for it. You are going to LIVE here, so tune up your surroundings to support your own individual psyche.

At this point you probably have a problem with regard to furnishings. Either you've got too much or you've got too little. Believe me, too much is worse. Trying to pack everything from a four-bedroom colonial into a one-bedroom trailer is an obvious impossibility, but believe me, people do try. My view is that furniture is clothing for houses, and if I'm truly going to strip down for relaxed naked living then I need to realize that all that "stuff," as George Carlin says, is just "shit!"

The worst possible solution is a huge storage locker, where you put out a hundred bucks or so every month like clockwork (which is as much as the rent on the place you are living!), and after two to five years or so sell, or junk, the sticks anyhow. If your kids or somebody else don't want it, either give it away to the Salvation Army or just plain dump it. If the kids start hopping up and down about Aunt Sophie's rocking chair, then ask them to pay the storage fees. You'd be surprised how quickly a simple suggestion like that will silence a good measure of tribal restlessness. I talk like it was easy, but what really happened is I did it wrong and wish I had spent the same money I wasted on storage for five years on a good bottle of wine or a dinner out each month instead. A bed or two, a solid dining-room table for entertaining, a few chairs, even folding ones, a couch for the living room for guest chats, and a bunch of bookshelves can be more than enough. If you enjoy putting together something more elegant and elaborate, fine, but I am simply making a list of what I have found to be basic and cheap, and above that the sky is the limit.

In fact, until I get settled in a place, a few filled U-Haul boxes with core doors or sheets of five-ply over them make great entertainment centers, end tables, free-form whatevers. With a bit of living in a place, things sort themselves out most of the time, and these temporary furnishings become superfluous, their contents move into bookshelves or other areas, and I can empty and knock down the boxes and not be burdened forever afterward by some cheap and ugly piece of veneered chipboard that becomes a useless space-taker or ankle-grabber.

Any time you think of adding another piece of wood and stuffing, pull out *Walden* and reread the passage where Henry David put all of his few furnishings out under the pines while he sprinkled and swept his cabin.[2]

Simplify, simplify, simplify. Not for puritanical reasons, but for personal freedom! You are living naked. Don't let too many things get in the way of your living. Paul said "a man's life doesn't consist of the things he owns." Too bad our Bible-thumping TV millionaire evangelists never got the message.

---

[2] *Walden or, Life In The Woods.* Thoreau, Henry David. New York: New American Library, 1960.

Moving can be a great experiment in keeping only what you want and need and getting rid of all the "stuff" or simply piling it up and enjoying sorting it out for yourself on a more measured basis.

I recently got tossed into the hospital, and after a fairly close call, reviewed where I was at "living naked." One thing that dawned on me was that the U-Haul boxes and stuff piled up in the hallway and bedrooms of my trailer would take me years to unpack and fuss over, and even then I probably could get along without most of the shit anyhow. As it was, there was a fair chance I wouldn't live that long, so one of my next projects was to contact a local auctioneer for a "household effects" auction and simply clear all that shit out in one swoop. Maybe I can leave at least one clear space in the universe when I die.

If, rather than having a whole store-full of furniture, you are moving into a nudist resort from a bare-bones apartment with practically nothing, your problems will be simpler, and your choices much wider.

The shit that's in the trailer you just bought was probably chosen by others of doubtful taste on a limited budget for temporary use, and they left it behind. If they didn't want it, why should you? Look it over carefully and feel really good about dumping the shit you don't like or will only maybe find a use for.

If in your case you are really coming out "bare bones" or all your stuff got lost in the fire or stolen by your spouse and his or her lawyers, you might aim for simple, modular, do-it-yourself furniture. I developed a flexible furniture style that includes the Paul Penhallow unpatented "string bed," a cheap, comfortable, novel, adjustable bed that can help your circulation and really allow you to relax, and a number of structurally supporting and functional modular bookshelves. Between the "string bed" working surfaces and the supporting bookshelves you can mix and match at will; since the units are free-standing, they can be moved around to suit any long-term or temporary interior functional needs you may have. Any time you get bored or need a different arrangement for a specific project, it is a simple manner to move things around or adjust levels and cover the bed with a core door or plywood sheet to temporarily convert your bed from an entertainment center into a work area, or vice versa. I routinely shift the position of the supporting bookshelves and my queen-size suspended bed on a seasonal basis to follow the rays of the rising sun from my bedroom window so that I continually get the pleasure of a naked stretch in the warm rays of "old Sol" every morning. If I ever locate the book I've been looking for on "Feng Shui,"[3] the oriental art of furniture placement in the greatest harmony with the Universe, this furniture will allow me to experiment to my heart's content.

The following integrated furniture design was developed over several years for modularity, flexibility, and comfort. It is simple to build from readily available parts, can be assembled in any small space, and disassembled for convenient transportation and reassembling at any new location. The major components are (first) sturdy bookshelves, (second) horizontal rope-supported work or resting surfaces, which can be desks, drawing boards, tables or beds, depending on their size and height adjustment. The key concept is that of the "string-bed" which allows convenient adjustment of the height of the working surfaces from low bed level to high drafting or art-work surface at any of several angles. (Third) a variety of progressively smaller modular separators and organizational dividers for books, papers, and files. All the furniture can be built from 1x12 finished pine boards for shelving, 1/4" interior plywood for bookshelf backing, 2x4 finished pine for support beams and bed and desk framing, 5/8" interior plywood for bed surfaces, two or three sizes of drywall screws, an electric drill with drill bits and drywall drivers, and a radial or Skil-saw.

The string beds are supported by substantial cross-beams placed on the ends of the bookshelves. The bookshelves are

[3] Flash! Just heard there is an article by Maggy Howe on Feng Shui, in the January, 1997, issue of *Country Living.*

completely free-standing, giving tremendous freedom in arrangement of beds to line up with existing windows and sources of sunlight as well as allowing for gradual seasonal changes to shift from winter solstice to equinox to summer solstice and back to fall equinox, if you want to keep in line with the highest sun peak each month. Or, if you are into magnetic orientations, you can say to hell with the walls and align the bed exactly to north or east according to your own persuasion.

The string bed also provides a gentle, supportive surface suspended in space in a practically frictionless manner. It takes a bit of practice to get over crashing it into the bookshelves or walls, but once you are used to centering yourself, sitting down rather than hopping sideways onto the bed, and then smoothly rolling from place to place rather than stomping about on all fours like a bull in a china shop, the string bed gives a "poor man's waterbed" that, to me is like napping on the deck of a small sailboat or large rowboat in a dead calm. Each movement of your own body is echoed in the feeling of suspension, gentle rocking and relaxation. The overall effect is one of true relaxation and gentle massage-like circulation. As the Chinese doctors say, there is only one disease, and that's congestion; and there is only one cure, and that is circulation. Perhaps the String Bed can contribute to your longer life and personal relaxation.

After you are tuned in to your own needs and your new digs, a long-term discriminating program of curb pickin's or dump scavenging can create wonders. You might take a look at *The Art & Science Dumpster Diving*[4] if you think you might enjoy that sort of diversionary adventure.

---

4 *The Art & Science Of Dumpster Diving*. Hoffman, John. Port Townsend, WA: Loompanics Unlimited, 1993.

Food

This can be a real challenge for a recently divorced dude who's never boiled water or a road warrior who's been gourmeting his way around the country on other people's money and just got off the train in Mobile on his own cash with no return ticket. The most favorable case is the self-employed worker or single mother who's used to making his or her own breakfast, packing their own lunches (for themselves and their kids) and taking supper out only part of the time. If you are a gourmet cook and disciple of Mr. Beardsley or Julia Childs, skip this section, it will probably make you ill.

There ain't no Micky D's on any nudist resort, so you'll have to feed yourself most of the time. (Although I just took a side trip from shopping and stopped at a pizza shop for a big one and a beer about 15 miles from the resort.) In my own search for food independence, I have developed a survival diet that works for me. The only appliances I need are a refrigerator (even a small one will do), a toaster oven, a coffee maker, and that infamous microwave oven.

My diet is based on supermarket commodity items, and I eat almost the same thing each day and thoroughly enjoy and savor every meal. My German mother-in-law used to say, "Hunger is the best cook," and with her cooking you needed it for most of her burnt offerings. When you cook for yourself you cook for your SELF.

In addition to your maintenance diet, you can look forward to weekly potlucks, club dinners and dances, barbecue and chili cook-offs, (and even a couple of resorts with upscale gourmet restaurants) for food (and social) variety. If you haven't yet discovered it, entertaining others can be gruesomely expensive, and it's not hard to blow a whole week's groceries on a two-hour potlatch at your place. Get smart. Invite everyone over for a potluck and make a casserole of creamed onions and carrots for the table. No sweat, no expense.

Buy a copy of *Joy of Cooking*, by Rombauer and Becker[5]. It's a teaching text and food survival guide all in one. I know few other places to get a good recipe for frozen octopus!

After 33 years of marriage, about 10 years of civil war and chaos, and one year of living naked, I just baked my first batch of oatmeal cookies. They tasted great! The recipe came right off the "gourmet" cookbook on the oatmeal box.

As you evaluate what works for you, remember to separate the cost of "food," i.e., nutrition, from the cost of booze, eating out, and other forms of entertainment that are sometimes mistakenly called "food."

As in any living-alone, self-employed or retired, no-time-clock lifestyle (now THERE is a concept), diet and health deserve special care and consideration. Even the seemingly boring, but necessary, health maintenance or personal-choice items such as your morning cup of coffee or daily shit, can give a welcome break and settled framework for the growth stuff.

Just remember: You are living naked and alone, so it's damned important to eat right and keep up your health. Being sick at a nudist park can be just as lonely and miserable as being sick in a high-rise ghetto, and out in the boonies, getting doctors can be a lot harder. Of course, if you have an exceptional mother who's more than happy to truck on down to the nudist camp with a big hot pot of chicken and matzo ball soup every time you come down with a head cold, more power to you!

Washing

Body hygiene is a natural wonder if you are living naked, what with a dip in the pool or shower and hot tub in the morning, another pool dip in the heat of the day, and a pre-night warm-up in the Ja-

---

[5] *Joy Of Cooking*. Rombauer, Irma S., Becker, Marion Rombauer. New York, Bobbs-Merrill Co., Inc. 1975.

cuzzi before retiring. Since your body isn't trapped in socks and shoes and underwear (including bras) and all the other layers of "armor" that society imposes upon us, your bodily energy isn't trapped or misdirected and poorly distributed, so you seldom sweat and yet hardly ever feel chill, and the mandatory soapy showers before using the pool and hot tub, the open fresh air, and moderate sunshine keep your skin and your whole bodily system feeling open and clean. Sometimes, when the water is shut off in a campground area for winter, for example, the hot showers, toilets, and Jacuzzi are still only a few steps away, with an occasional drying off in the sauna (if one is available) before returning to your own digs.

Clothing

Each to his or her own here. From cute matching sweatsuits for cool mornings to color-coordinated socks, shoes and sweatbands (and nothing else) for those tennis dates, the options are numerous. By and large, however, they are cheap.

My only attire on-site, year-round, is an old square of Pendleton blackwatch woolen material with a slot cut in the center to make a multifunctional poncho. Add to this a short length of rope as a belt (standard equipment for any nude guerrilla) to keep the breezes from blowing up the edges of the poncho and chilling my fanny, and I am all set for a short trek to the office or clubhouse, even when there is snow on the ground (which isn't too often here in south-central Virginia). Although nudists are often mistakenly called sun-worshippers, I find it more sensible to wear a broad-brimmed "Clint Eastwood" hat to keep the rain and sun off my head and face, which has already received more than its life-long share from living in the textile world. The rest of my Paris couture's outfit is a pair of self-ventilated tennis shoes I affectionately describe as my "$10 Birkenstocks." OK, I'm a fanatic. But it's fun!

Yeah, fun, but healthy, too. More and more research (not advertised by the textile world, of course) shows the adverse effects of constricting clothing,[6] [7] and the positive effects of exposure to sunlight.[8]

Most nudists aren't into Gucci, although on a cool morning at one of the upscale resorts you can often see bright, middle-aged couples taking their morning constitutionals in attractive matching L.L. Bean casual wear, followed most likely by a lone dude jog-trotting the same route with nothing on but his socks and Nikes. And no tan lines!

I must confess, however, to the ghost of Tom Molloy's *Dress for Success* that I do have at least one wash-and-wear, three-piece with a fine polka-dot tie — just for talking to bankers and lawyers.

Laundry

How much laundry need a nudist launder? My bi-weekly load is one set of bedding, a half-dozen or so towels, and one set of sweatshirt and wash pants for "town clothes." Since my clothes spend 90% of their lives neatly folded on the front seat of my car, you can see that my cleaning bill is no big deal. During the summer, the campground washer and dryer are available; one or two loads cost very little — and I can walk to and from the laundry area naked!

Haven't you ever had that fantasy of walking into your local laundromat, or going to your apartment's laundry room, and simply putting everything, including every stitch on your body, into the

---

[6] *Naked Beneath Our Clothing.* Veltheim, John. Union Hall, VA., PaRama, 1994. p 14.

[7] *Dressed To Kill: The Link Between Breast Cancer and Bras.* Singer, Sydney Ross and Soma Grismaijier. Garden City Park, NY: Avery Publishing Group, 1995.

[8] *Sunlight,* Zane R. Penryn, CA, World Health Publications, 1980.

washer? That fantasy is, for me, a daily reality, and can be yours also.

Transportation

This seems to be the one inescapable ball and chain of our society, and dependable transport is essential to independent survival for shopping, church (yes, Dorothy, some nudists do go to some churches), and other personal and maintenance errands. For all the glories of Avalon in Paw Paw, West Virginia, or White Tail Park in Ivor, Virginia, or many other fine resorts, let me give you a hint: "There ain't no commuter bus stops anywhere to be found, and the subway hasn't been dug yet."

Maintenance, in general

Living naked involves all the auto, mechanical, plumbing, electrical, appliance and other assorted ills a modern "Walden" is susceptible to. However, any group of nudists also contains a broad range of available talents. Ask around and give the right positive strokes all along the way. If it's a sink valve replacement, a refrigerator or water heater repair, or pulling your truck out of a bottomless pit, your nude neighbors, or the club owner (who has useful little things such as tractors and backhoes) are usually more than willing to help. If the job is major, some agreement about wages should be made ahead of time. In any case, it is typical farmer courtesy to offer to pay "whatever you think it's worth" for every task completed. The offer is nearly always refused, but universally appreciated as a sign that you care about the proper way to do things and will help to dull the shine of the "city slicker" label you might be wearing when you first move into your place. For more orientation on rural etiquette, and a book that's entertaining and instructive in its own right, I highly recommend Gene Logsdon's book, *The Contrary Farmer.*[9] It deserves a spot right beside your copies of *Walden* and *Sand County Almanac.*

In summary, your situation will probably develop along its own unique lines, but let's lay out what, after about two years of prospecting and development, I was able to come up with compared to what I had then.

Two years ago I was locked into a high-pressure teaching job at a state university. I lived in Syracuse, New York, where a typical winter's snowfall is somewhere between ten and twenty FEET of snow, with windchill factors not infrequently at forty or fifty below zero. I rented a two-room apartment on the 21st floor of a high-rise apartment building with no recreational facilities, a laundry room, and an outdoor pool that was useable only a few months of the year. The two-room apartment cost me $675 a month, with no equity and no cash value. My greatest memory of that place is looking out naked from my patio window one winter's day after one of our periodic "shut-down-the-world-for-36-inches-of-snow" blizzards and seeing below me on the Route 81 interstate one vehicle, a snowmobile, which appeared from somewhere north of there and kept on a perfectly straight bee-line southward until it was out of sight. I hope it gets to Florida, I said to myself, and started to seriously doubt my own sanity in staying in such an obviously hostile climate.

At this point, after the rapacious governor of New York State decided he would rather have my salary than my body, I have taken early retirement and am happily starving to death, holding my breath for the couple of years until my Social Security kicks in, living naked and enjoying it all. I live most of the time in the extra-wide trailer in Virginia with its three bedrooms, bath and a half, kitchen, dining and paneled living room with south-facing sliding glass doors. The resort has a 24-hour Jacuzzi, a Finnish sauna

---

9 *The Contrary Farmer.* Logsdon, Gene. Post Mills, VT, Chelsea Green Publishing Co., 1993.

which is cranked up on weekends, a summer outdoor swimming pool, tennis and volleyball courts, a clubhouse with two pool tables, weekly dances and potluck dinners, a nice walking path and nature trail, and is located in cotton and peanut country between the museums and theatre opportunities of the greater Norfolk area and, an equally easy drive in the other direction, historical colonial Williamsburg, and I can do all of it or none of it as I choose. The annual membership fees, together with full guest privileges, are presently $450, and the lease on the trailer site is $1,221 annually. My entire LP gas heat and electrical bills for this year have been around $350 for everything.

In addition, I am still hanging onto my first trailer in Pennsylvania. Membership there is $360, and the site lease is $1,200 per year. Since that trailer is used only for visits and as a fall-back if the Virginia summer gets too hot for me, and only briefly for cross-country skiing trips in the winter, or stopovers to entertain friends when traveling through that part of the country, the utilities bills have been minimal. This resort features two Jacuzzis (one indoor, one outdoor), tennis courts, sand-court volleyball, hiking trails, an exercise room and forced-hot-air sauna, an enclosed, heated swimming pool, snack bar and game room and lounge, large common sun deck and lawn, with a lovely creek running down through the property. The resort is convenient to the art and theatre activities of the Jim Thorpe and Bethlehem, Pennsylvania, arts and tourist areas, and has other local options for sailing, fishing, and hiking the Appalachian Trail, the Lehigh River Valley, and the Delaware Water Gap. All that, yet I spend most of my time there lying out naked in the shade on the big redwood deck suspended over the lawn. You don't have to do everything all at once.

By the way, these hints are mostly for your own guidance in getting to your own personal Nirvana. If you quote chapter and verse to any particular resort owner you might get any number of reactions, anywhere from a cold stare to a laugh, but most of which would be detrimental to the growth of your insider status. Be harmless as doves, but wise as serpents.

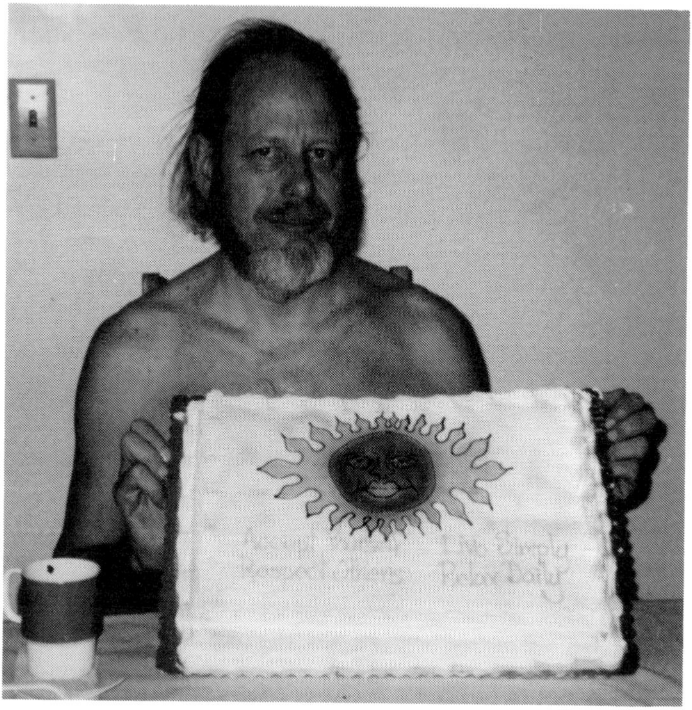

Paul Penhallow celebrating
his 60th birthday.

Chapter Five
Relax Daily

If you are the kind of independent, self-motivated person who would consider living naked, any detailed instructions on how you should live that life would be misdirected, to say the least, but a few observations might be in order.

We all wish fervently that the dominators and controllers would fuck off! Especially misguided owners and members who want to use the club as an arena for their egotistical suppression of other people's liberty. But if we can find a particular resort or group of people, including the owner, that we can get along with, we have a new world before us.

We are each, in some way, an artist, developing skills and creating something that is new, unique in the universe. August Rodin's studio in Paris was just such a center of artistic growth and experimentation (remember the lovely sculptures of "The Kiss" and "The Bronze Age")? Rodin hired a small group of nude models, not only to pose when asked to by himself and other artists in the studio, but just to live naked inside the studio so the artists could observe and become familiar with the nude form in all its unposed, natural, daily activities and situations. The fundamental basis of classical artistic training was drawing from the human figure, an activity which is presently continued only in a very few college courses within a busy curriculum and often carried out in semi-secrecy behind heavily curtained windows and doors. Perhaps this awareness of the fundamental artistic nature of the naked figure is the reason that a sketch book is well accepted in almost any gathering of nudists, and will quickly gather a small circle of admiring and interested people. This is in stark contrast to the nudist reaction to cameras. Cameras are, nearly universally, outlawed at nudist resorts, and any artistic photographer who wishes to pursue his interests while living naked will have many very difficult procedural difficulties to work out with the resort owner and the members of a particular club. Cameras are *verboten!*

If you are a good candidate for living naked, you can probably sit down and write out a brief description of three extremely valuable and important projects which you, as a professional person, have spent years chipping away at piece-meal with no discernible progress, but which you know down deep in your heart of hearts that you could finish off and have something really worthwhile if you just could get at it full time. Living naked is your chance to do just that. As an independent entrepreneur, consultant, artist, or craft person, you are well aware that an hour or two when you feel like doing a particular job can be worth weeks or months chained to the grindstone.

You also recognize the value of time out for relaxational procrastination. Such was the occasion for me one recent gray winter day. Winter, Virginia-style, narrows the options for that bit of relaxational procrastination to hiking (clothed for warmth, yuck) and hot tubbing (nude and natural, yummy).

I now get less exercise in cold weather than in summer, so I often substitute massage, either with friends or alone, to keep up circulation and flexibility. If you don't have access to a hot tub, you can use a sauna, or just empty all the unused costumes out of one of your un-clothes closets and install a towel-covered chair and a safe but powerful electric heater. Check with your doctor first, but then crank it up to about 150° F dry, if you are otherwise healthy, that is.

My massage routine, which you might try in the tub, is to rub and gently twist my toes and feet bones, working my way up the leg three times at different depths. First: Long surface strokes to flex the skin and move the venous circulation back toward the heart. Second: Kneading the muscles to purge out the waste products and bring in more oxygen and nutrients. Third: I finish with "fluffing" or gently pummeling the deep muscle areas. After finishing the legs, a few minutes of quite repose is great, especially when floating up to your neck in water at about 105° F! I suppose I could use the Jacuzzi jets, but doing the work myself also has benefits. Keeping the rest of my body as relaxed as possible while one hand or arm is performing the massage of some other part of the body is also good mental discipline. I have to be careful not to build tension back into my body while massaging, so I get out just as tense as I entered.

One wonderful result of hot tubbing is the "warm to the core" feeling that is very difficult to get from a regular bathtub, and to get really warn is impossible in a shower. After about 15 or 20 minutes of immersion, massage, and just plain relaxation in a hot tub, I can squeegee off most of the water with my hands, briskly rub off the few remaining droplets, and walk, practically glowing, back to my trailer, nude, with the outside temperature about 50° F. That feeling of relaxation and warmth will still be with me as I chose my next project, be it some daily routine, some new creation, or some other form of relaxation!

While you are looking for ways to expand your experience of living naked, you might also consider reaching out to touch someone via massage, and The Stroking Community[1]. Find your local group now; sign up for a workshop.

What does it feel like to be a member of The Stroking Community? Picture yourself lying on your back on a soft padded table in a warm, quiet room. A tape combining natural-sounding flutes and strings is playing quietly. Your eyes are closed and you feel quiet,

---

[1] Stroking Community Network, PO Box 279, Edisto Island, SC 29438

but a bit tense and stiff from a tough week at work. The first sense you have of your friends around you is a warm glow over your face as the leader's cupped hands above your face warm your brow and cheeks without touching them. The fingers gently, but firmly, make contact with your brow, and smooth and press away the worry wrinkles, lingering at your temples for a gentle circular rub, and then continue to sweep away the tension in your eyebrows, your cheeks, and your jaw line. The hands reach slowly under your head and, cradled carefully, your head floats effortlessly to the left, center, left again until your head is cradled in a warm hand and another hand is sweeping, carefully stretching out along your neck; over, around and back up under your shoulder, until the tension in your neck is warmed and relieved and softened away. As your attention moves from your shoulder you realize that for the past few minutes, you're not sure how long, both your feet and both your hands have been held and rubbed firmly with knuckles and thumbs and lovingly stretched and pressed until they are warm and relaxed with the increase in circulation and freedom of movement. As your head is gently placed back to center, that set of hands (or is it only one?) moves to your chest and you sense deep within a calmness as four other pairs of hands gently rest upon your wrists and ankles and then in a velvet-smooth, whisper-slow motion all five pairs of hands press gently and move up all four of your limbs and down your chest at exactly the same speed and pressure, moving together as one, as the warm, full, yet gentle pressure of the moving hands on your legs meets the hands moving in perfect unison over your chest and torso, and then they return. A few such sweeps, like the long ocean swells coming down a long, gradual beach, and your mind, imagination, and thoughts are set free, your worries and fears and tensions dissolve into the air, and you become one with the harmony of your body and the friends who are so lovingly and carefully communicating with you, personally, touchingly, warmly. You try to identify which hands are whose, but after a while you can't tell, and it matters not a bit as you simply trust and yield to the partnership of caring between all.

But that is only the beginning. There are coordinated wringing, kneading, rolling, even some lifting and bending of each limb to stretch out those tendons and flex those joints. After all this loving attention and active display of care, you lie there as the fingers, in a cycle of simultaneous sweeps, firmly then lightly massage both arms and both legs at the same time, moving fingertips from your thigh to your toes, your shoulder to your finger tips, all four limbs at the same time, and sweep once, twice, again, lighter and lighter, finally to an absolutely together, feather-light memory of complete relaxation and warmth and sharing. The group member who has been setting the pace and helping keep the team coordinated then applies a final, gentle, overall finishing stroke to emphasize the wholeness and unity of your body. A sheet is gently lifted up around you to keep you from catching a chill, and all ten hands rest warmly on your torso, your legs, your breasts, warmly and gently affirming their care, even through the separating fabric of the sheet.

But that isn't the end! After blissfully soaking in this feeling of trust and relaxation for a few minutes, you drop the sheet off, rather groggily, with assistance, turn over, and a similar sequence of rubs, and rolling, and gentle stretching multiplies the feeling of warm relaxation and divides the tensions and soreness of every square inch of your body into fine vapors that fade away leaving you with a feeling of complete peace and relaxation. Again you experience that coordinated sweep down your back and up each leg at the same time, with all the hands this time having a gentle conference on your buttocks before returning for another stroke. It is surprisingly diffuse, warm, like a mother's hug without the expected sexual titillation you might expect if you had not personally experienced it. The whole contact and body experience gives you an inexpressible feeling of pleasure, relaxation, warmth and security in the many, many loving hands of your friends.

After a brief rest, you sit up on the table and are enclosed in a big bear hug by all your group members before you have the joy and privilege of returning the favor and enjoy giving another member of your group the same blissful total relaxation you have just experienced. Physically and psychically, the experience is one of healing and healthy enjoyment.[2]

Of course, spending some of your nude time staying physically fit is as essential as it is relaxing. WARNING: You will as rarely find "Golds Gymnasium" in a nudist camp as you will find a nude body working out in the front windows of one of the downtown fitness centers. In some of the resorts you can look for or hope for some weights, an exercise bike, or other minor equipment. However, for the long run, you probably need to plan your regime using what you've got of your own. I have developed my own routine of stretches (called "Morning Song," no matter what time of day I enjoy it) that helps keep my muscles limber and my joints flexible. With the appropriate audience, I can even include a head stand!

Back in my younger days I enjoyed springboard diving as a competitive sport. Just try finding a nudist resort with a one-meter, much less a three-meter, diving board at the pool. The owner has heart failure at the very idea of what he would have to spring for in the way of insurance premiums! So I have given in to the textile world, sprung for "Speedos," and located the nearest public pool with an adequate board. I searched in vain for a source of swimming briefs that were not brilliant red, white, blue or satin black, swim wear that does not point a beacon to the sexually associated parts of the anatomy. Well, all right, some of us rebels would like to show that appearing to be nude (from a distance) is no big deal, and could serve as a first step in greater acceptance of the natural human body at beaches or parks. In 1990 I trained for the Empire

---

2 For a brief but insightful review of the personal philosophy of the founder of The Stroking Community, David Linton, see one of the sections of the video documentary, "Skinnydipping — U. S. A."

State Games at Green Lakes near Syracuse, and, at age 55, placed 11th in the state in the men's open division for ages 21 and older. In August, 1995, just weeks before my 60th birthday, I took first place in both one-meter and three-meter springboard diving in the Masters (age 50-59) division of the Games. Even though I had to go "out" to the Palmerton Swimming Pool from my "summer" home at Beechwood Lodge to train, I found the healthful and relaxing atmosphere of a nudist resort a healing contrast to the stress of conditioning and competing. Now my friends tease me about relaxing on my laurels!

While I lived in Syracuse, I opened my east-facing 21st floor apartment to members of the Syracuse Naturist Group. One schedule was based on Ben Franklin's habit of arising early and spending a naked hour or so reading and relaxing as his "air bath." I suggested arriving around 6:30 am, since a glorious preview of the sunrise often occurs about 15 minutes before the sun comes over the horizon. This brilliant sampler was usually followed by several minutes of "gray-time" to fix breakfast, select something to read or listen to, and get settled for the glories of the sunrise itself.

The full view of the eastern horizon was great, and the balcony was usable (with some prudence) in your natural state. Believe it or not, it was warm enough in the sun to bask comfortably outside even on rather cold days, and the large patio glass gave some sunspace inside most days. Old Sol quickly warmed up enough to enjoy a half hour or more of really relaxing sunbathing and reading before starting the work day.

Amazing where you can find space to relax daily, once living naked becomes your focus.

On the other end of the scale is the stereotypical retirement of the modern wage slave who works as long as he or she can on a dead-end job, paying ever more taxes and saving less and less year by year. These pitiful ghosts live in the same cage, with the same structure, the same constraints (including uncomfortable and expensive clothing) day to day in an environment which is totally noncondusive to original thought or constructive creativity. These empty souls depend on their jobs for any identity whatsoever, and their clothing is the false price of security they pay. So when they finally "retire" what do they do? Nothing. What happens then? Two to three years later they are dead.

What a contrast to someone who, while still active and alert, takes charge of his/her own finances and environment and starts building a REAL life.

As you contemplate plans for your REAL life, and the expenses of living it naked, consider assets other than your finances. At many nudist parks and resorts, it is not unusual for the owner to trade on-site work for some or all of your fees, especially if you are a permanent resident and are a dependable, hard worker. Personally, I now find I have too much of my own to do to get tangled in the endless list of local camp maintenance or service chores, and in the one case where I thought I had a deal worked out to trade some of my professional services for rent, it eventually fell through. Besides, keeping separate and just paying your way keeps that respectful distance between you and the owner which can help avoid misunderstandings, false expectations, and, eventually, an awkward parting of the ways. The boss may occasionally piss and moan or give a glimmer of a hint that he isn't totally happy about your lack of participation, but he knows which side his bread is buttered on and usually won't hassle you if you pay your bills on time and don't rub his nose in the fact that you may seem to be a bit standoffish.

Not all of us work in eight-to-five jobs, and thus have more experience in flexible hours and productively organizing time and life. There are many different reasons for living naked, and each of us, regardless of life style, may find a compatible group of friends at some nude resort. Some groups are specifically organized, as in any intentional community, around a certain theme. Gay clubs, AANR resorts, private clubs and lodges, all have their own individual personalities, but there are a few private resorts which have a special emphasis on health or political activism. Sometimes it takes a bit of sensitivity to discover these underground agendas, but if a particular resort is deeply committed to social justice, then you might get on board and enjoy it to the fullest. If you don't agree with that basic position, you will, of course, look for someplace else to live naked your own way.

The living out of your most basic needs for self-acceptance, respectful relationships, and simple existence can become a fantastic adventure, waking up and making breakfast naked, walking through the woods and down to a swimming pool where a couple of dozen naked folks are just lying out, enjoying the air, the sun, and the water. Just being with a bunch of people who, much more than the average, are willing to let you be yourself, because they have the self-acceptance to also be themselves, can take the pressure off your own spirit and allow you to grow in whatever way is best for you.

Many more things can come in their own time, but just deal with being naked first. You have become comfortable with your own body around your apartment, alone, but a larger social group of naked people can present a new situation.

Don't sweat it, act like one of the group, and in a surprisingly short time you will be accepted as part of the community. Opportunities to get involved will arise naturally, based on interests you have developed in your "spare time" over the years.

As a counter to the singles prejudice you met as a transient visitor, when you start living naked and become a permanent resident, the difficulties of acceptance will be much less. As a full-time resident at a resort you have many advantages. First, you are always there, so chances to develop friendships are much greater. If you do meet a friendly couple or the rare single gal, and you hit it off, you have someplace to entertain privately and, as they would say, "deepen the relationship." If you have some maturity and other talents or interests in art or writing or music, these can give you an edge over the other rootless single dudes who are just cruising through for a day or so. As a local, you can become familiar with the cultural and tourist attractions near your resort and provide information, or even offer to be a guide to off-site tourist attractions, art museums, or theaters. Owners have, by and large, made very little use of the attractions around their resorts which are of interest to their visitors. Yet, some of these clothed field trips or activities can be enhanced terrifically by either a full day relaxing naked, or some time after a dinner or theater date returning to the relaxing and comfortable environment of your resort.

If you hit it off with somebody outside the resort, then the pool, tennis courts, or hot tub can be a very strong attractant if you've got the courage to take a positive, "it's really great" attitude and invite your date out to "your place" for a visit.

Sex and nudity are so mangled together in our public psyche that it's only common sense to make your first invitation to visit at your nudist resort for a warm sunny afternoon rather than through the blue haze at 2 a.m. after last call at a local bar — but then again, if it works for you, go for it. Just make sure your shenanigans don't get you on the owner's shit list. He may be overjoyed to have your women friends around during the day but may not look as kindly on your touring all the local floozies through his joint during the wee hours. Besides, for security reasons, even your house guests will have to register, and depending on your membership fee set-up you may have to pay an additional day fee so he or she can use the rest of the club facilities. (Let me know if you find out a way to deduct this "nude evangelism" as a church-related expense.)

What more important and interesting challenge is there than sculpting your own life style according to your basic needs and full personal potential? Of course, this can best be done in an atmosphere of freedom, not repression; individuality, not conformity; responsibility, not wastefulness. Where, on the face of this earth as it is, can you find such an environment?

First, it won't be obvious or widely known.

Second, it may be difficult to get in.

Third, it may, surprisingly, be cheaper and more practical than you might imagine.

The place? A full-time nudist resort.

So now, you've bought your shed, moved your boxes into some back corner for leisurely unpacking, taken a last dip in the hot tub and a quiet stroll around the grounds, naked in the moonlight, before you lay down to sleep in your own bed, totally relaxed and at peace.

Good Goddess, it's quiet — no airplanes or throughways or city lights glaring all night into your space. Finally, after all your searching, work, and risk-taking you are truly living naked! You fall into the slumber of a newborn child. The next morning you awake refreshed, and walk, as nature intended, around your house, out your door, down the path to the pool or clubhouse — with the sun and air greeting and caressing your bare skin all over, and wearing nothing but, perhaps, some sandals, and carrying a towel comfortably curled behind your neck. Welcome.

Appendix I
The Options:
A Directory of Facilities

The following is a list of AANR (American Association for Nude Recreation)-affiliated parks, campgrounds, hotels and resorts, and does not include groups which do not own or lease grounds.

Alabama

Gymno-Vita Park
PO Box 121
Vandiver, AL 35176
205-672-7105

Sandstone Lodge
7501 Monroe Lane
Mobile, AL 36613
205-645-0536

Arizona

Jardin del Sol
PO Box 39
Marana, AZ 85653
520-682-2537

California

Desert Shadows Inn
260 Chuckwalla Rd
Palm Springs, CA 92262
619-325-6410
800-292-9298

Elysium Fields
814 Robinson Rd
Topanga, CA 90290
310-455-1000

Glen Eden Sun Club
PO Box 641
Corona, CA 91718
909-277-4650
800-843-6833

La Petit Chateau
1491 Via Soledad
Palm Springs, CA 92264
619-325-2686

McConville
PO Box 477
Lake Elsinore, CA 92531
909-678-2333

Olive Dell Ranch
26520 Keissel Rd
Colton, CA 92324
909-825-6619

Sequoians Family Nudist Park
PO Box 2095
Castro Valley, CA 94546
415-582-0194

Terra Cotta Inn
2388 E. Racquet Club Rd
Palm Springs, CA 92262
619-327-1504
619-322-6059

Laguna del Sol
8683 Rawhide Lane Box 1
Wilton, CA 95693
916-687-6550

Lupin Naturist Club
20600 Aldercroft Heights Rd
Los Gatos, CA 95030
408-353-2250

Morningside Inn
888 N. Indian Canyon
Palm Springs, CA 92262
619-325-2668

Raffles Palms Springs Hotel
280 Mel Ave
Palm Springs, CA 92262
619-320-3949

Silver Valley Sun Club
48382 Silver Valley Rd
Newberry Springs, CA 92365
619-257-4239

Treehouse Nudist Resort
1924 Glen Helen Rd
Devore, CA 92407
909-887-7056

Colorado

Mountain Air Ranch
8796 S Mica Mine Gulch Rd
Littleton, CO 80127
303-697-4083

Connecticut

Solair Recreation League
PO Box 187
Southbridge, MA 01550
203-928-9174

Florida

Club Paradise at
Paradise Lakes
PO Box 750
Land O'Lakes, FL 34639
813-949-9327
800-237-2226 Outside FL

Cypress Cove
4425 S Pleasant Hill Rd
Kissimmee, FL 34746
407-933-5870

Ethos Trace, Inc.
PO Box 2233
Pace, FL 32571
904-994-3665

Gulf Coast Resort
13220 Houston Ave
Hudson, FL 34667
813-868-1061

The Island Group
PO Box 397
Land O'Lakes, FL 34639
813-996-3289

Lake Como Club, Inc
20500 Cot Rd
Lutz, FL 33549
813-949-1810

Riverboat Club
PO Box 56
2500 Carriker Rd
Land O'Lakes, FL 34639
813-996-6008

Seminole Health Club
3800 S. W. 142nd Ave
Davie, FL 33330
305-473-0231

Sunburst Resort
2375 Horn Road
Milton, FL 32570
904-675-6807
904-675-3067

Sunnier Palms
Members' Lodge
8800 Okeechobee Rd
Fort Pierce, FL 34945
407-468-8512

Sunny Sands Resort
502 Central Blvd.
Pierson, FL 32180
904-749-2233

Sunsport Gardens
14125 North Rd
Loxahatchee, FL 33470
407-793-0423

Georgia

Bell Acres Recreation Enterprise, Inc.
PO Box 302
Maysville, GA 30558
706-677-2931

Hidden Valley
Rt 3 Box 3452
Dawsonville, GA 30534
706-265-6110

Mountain Creek Grove
PO Box 3197
Cleveland, GA 30528
706-865-6930

Serendipity Park, Inc.
95 Cedar Hollow
Cleveland, GA 30528
706-219-3993

Idaho

Bare Backers
PO Box 5781
Boise, ID 83705
208-322-6853

Illinois

Blue Lake, Inc.
PO Box 13
Erie, IL 61250

Indiana

Fern Hills Club
7330 South Rockport Rd
Bloomington, IN 47403
812-824-4489

Lake O'The Woods Club, Inc.
PO Box 53
Valparaiso, IN 46384
219-477-6643
219-462-9376

Sunny Haven Recreation Park
PO Box 100
Granger, IN 46530
219-277-5356

Tri-State Country Club, Inc.
79 DrakesRidge
Bennington, IN 47011
812-427-3914

Kansas

Prairie Haven
Rt 1, Box 169A
Scranton, KS 66537
913-793-2738

Sandy Lane Club, Inc.
PO Box 1866
Hutchinson, KS 67504
316-543-2645

Louisiana

La Pines Ranch
29414 Cyprian Drive
Lacombe, LA 70445
504-882-5662

Maryland

Pen-Mar Club
PO Box 276
Hancock, MD 21750
717-294-3262 Weekends

Pine Tree Associates, Inc.
PO Box 195
Crownsville, MD 21032
410-841-6033

Massachusetts

Renaissance Resorts, Inc.
PO Box 504
West Stockbridge, MA 01266
413-232-7860

Sandy Terraces Associates
PO Box 98
Marstons Mills, MA 02648
508-428-9209

Michigan

Forest Hills
PO Box 105
Saranac, MI 48881
616-642-9526

Sunshine Gardens Resort
21901 Collier Ave
Battle Creek, MI 49017
616-962-1600

Turtle Lake Resort
2101 Nine Mile Rd
Union City, MI 49094
517-741-7004

Whispering Oaks, Inc.
5864 Baldwin Rd
Oxford, MI 48371
810-628-7200

Minnesota

Avatan, Inc.
PO Box 580950
Minneapolis, MN 55458
612-434-4922

Oakwood Club, Inc.
PO Box 65147
St. Paul, MN 55165

Missouri

Forty Acre Club
PO Box 309
Lonedell, MO 63060
314-629-0050
314-629-9916

New Jersey

Rock Lodge Club
PO Box 86
Stockholm, NJ 07460
201-697-9721

New York

Buckridge
215 Tuttle Hill Rd #2
Candor, NY 13743
607-659-3868

Empire Haven
Rt 3, Box 297
Moravia, NY 13118
315-497-0135

Full-Tan Sun Club
Rt 1 Box 34
Sprakers, NY 12166
518-673-2886

North Carolina

Bar-S Ranch
Rt 2, Box 402
Reidsville, NC 27320
919-349-2456

Whispering Pines
1114 Sun Street
Shallotte, NC 28452
910-287-6404

Ohio

Alpine Resort
120 Fell Avenue
Northfield, OH 44067
216-674-6856
216-467-4658

Cedar Trails
11 Cow Run Rd
Peebles, OH 45660
513-764-1365

Green Valley
PO Box 740
Bath, OH 44210
216-659-3812

Paradise Gardens
6100 Blue Rock Rd
Cincinnati, OH 45247
513-385-4189

Sunn Jammers
Recreational Park
3207 Brownsville Rd, SE
Newark, OH 43055
614-763-4217

Oklahoma

Oaklake Trails
PO Box 470564
Tulsa, OK 74147
918-455-8120

Sun Meadow
PO Box 521068
Tulsa, OK 74152
-266-7651

Oregon

Restful Haven Health Club
PO Box 248
North Plains, OR 97133
503-647-2449

Squaw Mountain Ranch
PO Box 4452
Portland, OR 97208
503-630-6136

Willamettans, Inc.
PO Box 969
Marcola, OR 97454
503-933-2809

Pennsylvania

Beechwood Lodge
PO Box 5
Ashfield, PA 18212
717-386-4449

Broken Arrow
Rt 1 Box 266-D
Polk, PA 16342
814-432-8606
412-652-2641

Penn Sylvan Health Society
Rt 3, Box 3770
Mohnton, PA 19540
717-445-6330

Sunspot
PO Box 211
Susquehanna, PA 18847
717-853-3060

White Thorn Lodge
383 State Line Rd
Darlington, PA 16115
412-846-5984

Rhode Island

Dyer Woods Nudist Campground
114 Johnson Rd
Foster, RI 02825
401-397-3007
401-392-3064

South Carolina

Carolina Foothills
PO Box 657
Chesnee, SC 29323
803-461-2731

Cedar Creek
260 Gantt Mill Rd
Leesville, SC 29070
803-894-5159

Remick's Haven
9 Remicksville Drive
Cleveland, SC 29635
803-836-3447

Sunair Health Club
Rt 1, Box 126-L
Graniteville, SC 29829
803-663-6377

Tennessee

Cherokee Sun Lodge
PO Box 2897
Crossville, TN 38557-2897
615-277-5140

Rock Haven Lodge, Inc.
PO Box 1291
Murfreesboro, TN 37133
615-896-3553

Timberline Lodge Resort
PO Box 1173
Crossville, TN 38557
800-TAN-NUDE

Texas

Bluebonnet
Rt 1, Box 146
Alvord, TX 76225
817-627-2313

Live Oak Ranch
Rt 1, Box 916
Washington, TX 77880
409-878-2216

Natural Horisun
PO Box 809
Needville, TX 77461
409-884-0415

Riverside Resort
PO Box 14413
San Antonio, TX 78214
210-393-2387

Sandpipers Holiday Park
Rt 7, Box 309
Edinburg, TX 78539
210-383-7589

Sunny Pines Nudist Ranch
PO Box 133
Wills Point, TX 75169
903-865-1521
903-873-3311

Vista Grande
1149 FM 1185
Weatherford, TX 76086
214-288-1104
817-598-1312

Vermont

Forest City Lodge, Inc.
260 Beebe Hill Rd
Milton, VT 05468
802-893-4513

Virginia

White Tail Park
PO Box 160
Zuni, VA 23898
804-859-6123

Washington

Fraternity Snoqualmie
PO Box 748
Issaquah, WA 98027
206-392-6833

Kaniksu Ranch
4295 N Deer Lake Rd #5
Loon Lake, WA 99148-9650
509-233-8202

Lake Associates
Recreation Club, Inc.
PO Box 654
Conway, WA 98238
360-424-6833

Lake Bronson Club
PO Box 1135
Sultan, WA 98294
206-793-0286

West Virginia

Avalon
PO Box 369
Paw Paw, WV 25434
304-947-5600

Wisconsin

Valley View Recreation Club
PO Box 605
Cambridge, WI 53523
608-423-3060 Weekends

Campgrounds sometimes close, and new resorts are springing up around the country. For information about such changes contact:

American Association for Nude Recreation
1703 N. Main Street
Kissimmee, FL 34744-3396
800-879-6833
(That's an easy phone number to remember: 800-TRY-NUDE)

In addition to parks and clubs which are part of AANR, there are many unaffiliated facilities, one of which could be YOUR Shangri-La. If you are just beginning your adventures in living naked, you may want to try a local skinny-dipping spot, or a nude beach where you'll meet folks who know about these things. Information about nude beaches and areas that are known as skinny-dipping spots can be obtained from:

The Naturist Society
PO Box 132
Oshkosh, WI 54902

If you are interested in information about the growing number of clothing-optional facilities specifically for gay men, a list of affiliated clubs is available from:

GNI (Gay Naturists International)
PO Box 7150
Corte Madera, CA 94976
or
Gay Nude Guide
Summers Edge Studios, Inc.
757 SE 17th St #3071
Fort Lauderdale FL 33316
305-764-6162

Appendix II
Bibliography:
A *Barely* Sufficient Library

My *Barely Sufficient Library* begins with a full set of the *Encyclopedia Brittanica* (24 volumes plus the one-volume atlas and the three-volume dictionary) and is one reason I need a five ton truck for traveling further than the local grocery store. The following list is an example of volumes that have directly influenced my ***Living Naked And Frugal***. You, of course, must develop your own particular inspirational sources for your new adventures into the freedom of living naked.

Browne, Harry. *How I Found Freedom In An Unfree World.* New York: Avon, 1973.

Budge, E. A. Wallis. *The Book Of The Dead.* New York: Penguin Books, 1989.

Carnegie, Dale. *How To Win Friends And Influence People.* New York: Simon and Schuster, 1964.

Franklin, Benjamin. *Autobiography.* New York: Charles E. Merrill, 1918.

Hartman, William E., Marilyn Fithian and Donald Johnson. *Nudist Society.* New York: Crown Publishers, Inc., 1970.

Hoffman, John. *The Art & Science Of Dumpster Diving.* Port Townsend, WA: Loompanics Unlimited, 1993.

Jefferson, Thomas. *The Portable Thomas Jefferson.* (Edited and with introduction by Merrill D. Peterson.) New York: Viking Press, 1974.

Johnson, Donald. *The Nudists.* Spokane, WA: Outdoor American Corporation, 1959.

Kime, Zane R. *Sunlight.* Penryn, CA: World Health Publications, 1980.

Lee Baxandall's World Guide To Nude Beaches And Resorts. Oshkosh, WI: N EDITIONS, 1995.

Li Yu, translated by Patrick Hanan. *The Carnal Prayer Mat.* New York: Ballantine Books, 1990.

Logsdon, Gene. *The Contrary Farmer.* Post Mills, VT: Chelsea Green Publishing Co., 1993.

Merrill, Frances and Mason. *Among The Nudists.* Garden City, NY: Garden City Publishing Co., 1931.

Musashi, Miyamoto. *A Book Of Five Rings.*(Translated by Victor Harris.) Woodstock, NY: Overlook Press, 1982.

North American Guide To Nude Recreation, 18th Edition. Kissimmee, FL: American Sunbathing Association, Inc., 1993.

Paine, Thomas. *Common Sense.* (Edited, with introduction by Isaac Kramnick.) New York: Penguin Books, 1986.

Rogers, Carl. *On Becoming A Person; A Therapist's View Of Psychotherapy*. Boston: Houghton Mifflin, 1961.

Rombauer, Irma S., and Marion Rombauer Becker. *Joy Of Cooking*. New York: Bobbs-Merrill Co., Inc., 1975.

Rubaiyat Of Omar Khayam. Rendered into English Verse by Edward Fitzgerald. A. L. Burt Company, Publishers.

Schacter-Shalomi, Zalman, and Ronald S. Miller. *From Age-ing To Sage-ing*. New York: Warner Books, 1995.

Singer, Sydney Ross and Soma Grismaijer. *Dressed To Kill: The Link Between Breast Cancer And Bras.* Garden City Park, NY: Avery Publishing Group, 1995.

Strange, Julian. *Adventures In Nakedness.* New York: Alfred A. Knopf, 1934.

Sun-Tzu. *The Art Of War.* (Translated by Samuel B. Griffith.) New York: Oxford Press, 1963.

Teter, George. *One Hundred Narrative Poems.* Chicago: Scott, Foresman and Company, 1918.

Thoreau, Henry David. *Walden Or, Life In The Woods And On The Duty Of Civil Disobedience.* New York: New American Library, 1960.

Tillich, Paul. *The Courage To Be.* London: The Fontana Library, Sixth Printing, 1969.

VanderBroeck, Goldian, ed. *Less Is More; The Art Of Voluntary Poverty.* New York: Harper and Row, 1978.

Veltheim, John. *Naked Beneath Our Clothing*. Union Hall, VA: PaRama, 1994.

Whitman, Walt. *Poems From Leaves Of Grass.* New York: E. P. Dutton & Co., 1913.

YOU WILL ALSO WANT TO READ:

☐ **17079 TRAVEL-TRAILER HOMESTEADING UNDER $5,000,** ***by Brian Kelling.*** Tired of paying rent? Need privacy away from nosy neighbors? This book will show how a modest financial investment can enable you to place a travel-trailer or other RV on a suitable piece of land and make the necessary improvements for a comfortable home in which to live. This book covers cost break-down, tools needed, how to select the land and travel-trailer or RV, and how to install a septic system, as well as water, power (including solar panels), heat and refrigeration systems. ***1995, 5½ x 8½, 80 pp, illustrated, indexed, soft cover.*** **$8.00.**

☐ **17056 FREEDOM ROAD,** ***by Harold Hough.*** Have you dreamed about leaving the rat race but don't know where to start? This book will show you how to make a plan, eliminate your debts, and buy an RV. You'll learn about beautiful places where you can live for free. You'll learn how to live a comfortable, healthy lifestyle on just a few dollars a day. Why wait for retirement when you can live a low-cost, high travel lifestyle today? ***1991, 5½ x 8½, 174 pp, illustrated, soft cover.*** **$16.95.**

☐ **85103 GENITOLOGY,** ***by Dr. Seymore Klitz & Dr. Ima Peeper.*** Some people read palms, some read tea leaves, some read the bumps on your head. Some people read this book and really have fun. The History of Genitology; How to Do a Correct Reading for Males; How to Do a Correct Reading for Females; How to Interpret the Readings. Both male and female genitalia are thoroughly covered... er, uncovered... in this amazing book. Highly recommended for anyone going into the area of genitals. ***1983, 5½ x 8½, 126 pp, abundantly illustrated, soft cover.*** **$10.00.**

☐ **85225 A MAN'S GUIDE TO ADVERTISING FOR A WOMAN,** ***by Sebastian Phillips.*** Men! Are you desperately seeking a woman... or would you like to? Then this book is a must! It explains how to properly structure "Personals" ads that will attract not one, but many women. Learn where, when and why to place your ads, buzzwords that get results, the do's and don'ts of composition, how to screen your responses, and how to stack the odds in your favor so that the war between the sexes comes to a screeching halt and love and courtship prevail. This is the best book ever written on the subject. ***1996, 5½ x 8½, 184 pp, illustrated, soft cover.*** **$16.95.**

Loompanics Unlimited
PO Box 1197
Port Townsend, WA 98368

LN7

Please send me the books I have checked above. I have enclosed $____________ which includes $4.95 for shipping and handling of the first $20.00 ordered. Add an additional $1 shipping for each additional $20 ordered. Washington residents include 7.9% sales tax.

Name ____

Address ______________________________________

City/State/Zip __________________________________

VISA and MasterCard accepted. 1-800-380-2230 for credit card orders *only*.
8am to 4pm, PST, Monday through Friday.